SPORT IN SOCIETY

BY

P. C. McINTOSH

LONDON
C. A. WATTS & CO. LTD.
1963

First published 1963

©

P. C. McIntosh
1963

PRINTED IN GREAT BRITAIN IN THE CITY OF OXFORD
AT THE ALDEN PRESS
36/604

TO

A. D. M.

CONTENTS

PLATES

(Between pages 104 and 105)

I

INTRODUCTORY:
POINTS OF CONTACT

WHY is each celebration of the Olympic Games separated by
an interval of four years? Consideration of this specific
question may serve to introduce the complex subject of this
book better than could definitions of sport and of society.
The organization of an Olympic Festival includes nowadays
the provision of elaborate facilities for sixteen sports or more,
the building of a "village" for competitors and officials from
eighty or ninety different countries, the arrangement of transport and communication through the Press, broadcasting and
television, and the establishment of services for the health,
welfare, nourishment, and entertainment of many thousands
of spectators. The whole process costs vast sums of money and
takes about six years. Even with a four-year interval between
each Olympic Festival preparations for two festivals now
overlap. Four years may well be a convenient period of
intermission, but convenience was not the reason for it.

Baron Pierre de Coubertin, in founding the modern
Olympic Games at Athens in 1896, drew much of his inspiration from the ancient Olympic Festivals which German
archaeologists and scholars unearthed and popularized in the
nineteenth century. The ancient games were held every four
years and we are, therefore, at once transported back to 776
B.C., and many years before that date, to find the origin of
the festival and the four-year cycle which we still observe.

In historic times the Olympic Games were an intrinsic part
of a religious festival in honour of the god Zeus. The five-day
programme included sacrifices and religious rituals as well as
races, wrestling, and competitions in the arts. Some scholars

have maintained that the association of religion with competitive sport was to a great extent haphazard. A religious festival provided the concourse of people and so the occasion for races and contests. One of the legends woven round the Games told how they were originally funeral games in honour of the hero Pelops. Certainly funeral games were features of early Greek culture. The games organized at the funeral of Patroclus were described in great detail by Homer in the *Iliad* and had their counterparts on other like occasions. There were, however, other details of the legend about Pelops and other features of the festival in historic times which suggest a deeper significance in the association of sport with religion.

Pelops was a Phrygian who came to central Greece and there challenged Oenomaus, King of Pisa, to a chariot race which Oenomaus had ordained as the trial for the hand of his daughter Hippodamia. Oenomaus was thrown and killed in the race and Pelops took his daughter and his kingdom. Sir James Frazer and F. M. Cornford suggested that Pelops the victor in the chariot race, was the lineal descendant of the divine king or weather magician. His title to the kingdom depended on a contest and he had periodically to defend his title. Belief in mimetic magic credited the victor with power to bring fertility and growth to crops and stock. In historic times the Olympic festival always took place at the second or third full moon after the summer solstice. The movements of the sun and moon may well have determined the time of early races for fertility and kingship. Even today the failure of the solar year to coincide with lunar months is occasionally thrust upon our notice, but every eight years they do coincide. Eight solar years are approximately equal to ninety-nine lunar months. The Olympic Festival was celebrated every fiftieth and forty-ninth month, on a date which thus always fell by our reckoning between 6th August and 19th September.

Our first record of a victor at Olympia has been dated 776 B.C. but there is little doubt that festivals and contests were held there in 1300 B.C. or earlier and with the disappearance of Neolithic culture and the growth of cities and civilization it is not surprising if the Greeks of the seventh and sixth centuries B.C. had lost sight of the original religious significance of the races except in so far as it was enshrined in legend and ritual.

There is no certainty about the religious origin of athletic competition in Greece but anthropological researches as far apart as Ireland and Bali have tended to emphasize the importance of mimetic magic in primitive societies. The dead are often identified with powers of growth and, just as blood shed by means of sacrifices was thought to refresh the dead for their labours, so the degree of vigour expended in sport was thought to be transferred to the powers of growth and fertility. Today sacrifices and athletic contests have been replaced as agricultural and biological instruments yet there is a curious echo of primitive beliefs in the strivings of the nation states to indicate their vitality through their success in international sport and in the sense of shame and humiliation which the sporting Press reveals when athletes or footballers fail to justify the hopes and expectations of the masses.

The ancient Olympic Games, according to an historian of the eleventh century, Cedrenus, ceased in the reign of Theodosius the Great between A.D. 392-395 Theodosius II in a vigorous campaign for the suppression of paganism in favour of Christianity decreed in A.D. 408 that all pagan temples and images should be destroyed. The temple of Zeus at Olympia was burned and it would have been difficult for the Olympic festival to continue. The beginning and the end of the Olympic Games were thus determined by current religious thought and practice.

The Olympic Games provide perhaps the best documented

evidence of the association of competitive sport with religion. There are many other examples in histories of primitive societies and early civilizations. The Tailtenn Games in Ireland, wrestling among the Aztecs, the team game of Thlachtli played by Maya people in central America, and ju-jitsu practised by the Samurai warriors of Japan, all had religious significance. In Britain, too, the early history of some games of football suggests that fertility rites were involved. At Inveresk in Scotland there was formerly a match between the married and unmarried women, and in Scone a game between bachelors and married men. Christmas was the traditional festival time when these were played.

Ritual is still a need of modern man even in his sport. The modern Olympic Games, with their torch-bearers' relay, unfurling of flags, victory celebrations and national anthems are crowded with rituals. The setting of a flag on the summit of Everest and the saying of a prayer by Sherpa Tensing result from a similar need for ritual. At the Cup Final at Wembley community singing quickly became ritual and since 1928 when "Abide with me," Queen Mary's favourite hymn, was first sung, this deeply religious expression of man's nature has been the climax of the pre-match ritual—a climax so moving that it cannot fail to make the most impassive atheist ponder its significance.

Throughout the last two thousand years religious observance and competitive sport have constantly impinged upon each other. In more recent years the association between religion and sport has become both more sophisticated and more pragmatical than it was. The Harrow School song "Forty Years On" pleads—

> God give us bases to guard or beleaguer
>   Games to play out, whether earnest or fun:
> Fights for the fearless and goals for the eager
>   Twenty and thirty and forty years on!

Religion, however, has not always been the friend and ally of sport. Sunday observance has been the aim of voluntary societies and was the object of Acts of Parliament in 1677 and 1871. It probably helped to prevent sport from developing for the industrialized inhabitants of towns and cities until social and economic progress made the twelve o'clock Saturday a feature of life in Britain.

Economic development, prosperity and poverty have been important in shaping the pattern of sport in a community. Britain pioneered the Industrial Revolution and during the nineteenth century was first in the field with a pattern of sport for an industrial and urban population. Neither the Football Association (1863) nor the Amateur Athletic Association required the preceding designation "British" or even "English." There were no other like associations. Earlier than these two associations came the "Alpine Club" (1859), again needing no national designation. This was the more remarkable in that its activities were necessarily carried on in other nations' territories. At first there were no rivals and it has been left to other national clubs and associations to distinguish themselves from the British.

These three sporting groups, the footballers, the athletes and the mountaineers, were drawn, one hundred years ago, from the middle class. This class rose to a position of political power and social influence on the crest of the wave of industrial development. They shaped their games and sports to a large extent at the Public Schools. Most of these schools were new or reformed boarding schools catering for a clientele that aspired to the position and privilege of those who had already passed through Eton, Harrow, Winchester and the few other long-established schools of national repute. The geographical situation of the new schools often depended on the new network of railways which spread rapidly across Britain from 1830. Marlborough College under its headmaster Cotton, rather than Rugby School under Arnold, was the real pioneer of games and sports as instruments in education. Marlborough College, founded in 1842, was also one of the first "railway schools" drawing its pupils from homes far afield and its supplies from centres well beyond the effective range of horse and cart.

Sport for the working classes came later than for the middle classes. In a detailed study of Birmingham and district D. D. Molyneux has shown conclusively that sport there grew when Saturday became a general half-holiday. For most workers this resulted from victory in its campaign for a nine-hour day. The campaign was fought and won between 1869 and 1873, years of great prosperity for Birmingham and for the country as a whole.

It was not many years before some areas of sport were heavily commercialized. This was particularly true of football. A certain level of economic development is essential before professionalism can be supported. This was as true of the Mediterranean world of imperial Rome as it has been true of Britain and the United States during the last hundred years and of Russia during the last twenty-five.

The economic importance of sport lies not merely in its absorption of surplus wealth and leisure. In modern societies the financial structure of a country may use sport as an important supporting member. Sport with its ancillary or attendant industry of gambling provides the national exchequer with a considerable income. In Norway, for instance, science as well as sport is financially assisted with revenue taken directly from gambling on sport. In Britain the revenue from football pools, some £30,000,000 in 1961–2, goes to the general exchequer revenue.

Social and economic structure are not easy to separate but there are many instances of social structure being reflected in sport or perhaps being reinforced by it. The Olympic Games were, of course, open to free-born Greeks only. The whole civilization of the Greek city states depended on the institution of slavery. Slaves were denied participation in sport and on them depended the possibility of freedom for free-born athletes to train for ten months before each festival. To the citizen of Rome the Greek athletic festival never made a strong appeal even when sponsored by the Emperor himself. Greece was conquered during the second century B.C. The athletic pursuits of the conquered race, then rapidly being dominated by professional athletes, had little to commend them to the conquerors. On the other hand the Romans encouraged and pushed forward the commercialization of sport throughout the Mediterranean world.

In the history of Europe the sports of those who were politically powerful and socially privileged were usually clearly distinguished from the sports of the rest of the population. The tournament which in the thirteenth century was a serious form of military training for knights and their esquires became a stylized and decorative pastime for the nobility of the fifteenth. The humanist educators of the Renaissance specifically distinguished noble from ignoble sports in describing the conduct of a courtier and the education of the young. John Locke advocated fencing and riding because they were "looked upon as so necessary parts of breeding that it would be thought a great omission to neglect." From a strictly utilitarian point of view Locke would have preferred wrestling to fencing. Positive requirements have had their negative counterparts. An old Etonian of the mid-nineteenth century wrote that "football was a game fit for butcher boys," and a headmaster condemned the same sport and added, as a summary condemnation, "why, the Yorkshire common people play it."

Nobility has been apparent not merely in the selection of sports but in the manner of their performance. The Renaissance upheld *gratia* and *sprezzatura* (disdain) in performance. Ostentation was to be avoided. "Gentlemanly conduct" is still enshrined in the Laws of Football and is a survival of a social code inseparable from the social structure of nineteenth-century England. Sporting costume also during the nineteenth century betrayed social distinctions. In the early years of the century men throughout Europe adopted English riding costume. The ideal of gentility made every man want to look like an English country gentleman whose dress was in part determined by his sports and pastimes. The stove-pipe hat originally designed to protect the head of the hunting man was worn by fishmongers, policemen, cricketers, and the Oxford and Cambridge crews even when rowing. The blazer, too, was originally a sporting uniform denoting gentility—a distinction which it lost as it became more generally adopted.

Gentlemanly conduct in sport, then, had its sartorial side. It also signified a moral code and indeed the nineteenth century was a period when many words and phrases from sport found their way into more general usage. Nearly all of them had an ethical connotation. Phrases which came into general usage in earlier centuries like "cut out for it," taken from cock-fighting, rarely had moral implications. On the other hand "play the game," "it's not cricket," "hitting a man when he is down," "no holds barred," "fair play," "below the belt," and many others, all suggested an ethic which was generally understood. They show that sport was closely integrated in the life of the people. Such phrases are now less commonly used than formerly and perhaps sport has less of a moral flavour than once it had, but "fair" and "fair play" have achieved a remarkable ubiquity. The words themselves are to be found in Low German and Danish and other languages and dialects. They can be heard in French political life and in big-business transactions on both sides of the Atlantic Ocean.

Sport no less than art and literature is bound up with the moral code and the values of a community. In the age when the Olympic Games flourished some Greek city states practised infanticide of weaklings. Both Plato and Aristotle stated categorically that medical treatment should not be wasted on those whose condition would prevent them becoming useful to society. Sport was for the fit and only for the fit. This attitude contrasts fiercely with modern social policy on the care of the injured. The exercise of compassion has led to large sums of public and private money being spent upon the education and recreation of the physically handicapped and upon the rehabilitation of the injured, many of whom will never be very useful to society nor will repay the care that has been given to them. In Rome after the Olympic Games of 1960 a second series of competitions was held for the disabled. Four hundred paraplegic competitors from twenty-one countries assembled for swimming, archery, fencing, throwing events, table tennis, and basket-ball played by teams in wheel chairs. Clearly in this setting sport was no longer, if it ever had been, merely an instrument of rehabilitation; it was rather a satisfaction and an end in itself which the handicapped were entitled to achieve in the fullest measure possible to them.

Sport, like other spheres of human activity, has its political aspect, yet in some countries the pretence that sport is non-political is still kept up. It is doubtful whether the proposition that sport is non-political has even been true since the time when Pelops defeated Oenomaus in a chariot race and took his kingdom as part of the prize. It was certainly not true when Sparta used victories at the Olympic Games as tests of her vitality and prestige, nor when an anxious imperial government provided for the citizens of Rome elaborate facilities for physical recreation and sport, nor when football was suppressed in England in favour of archery, nor when the

Nazi Government of Germany utilized the Olympic Games in 1936 for political ends, nor when the British Government sent Roger Bannister on a propaganda tour of the United States after he had first run a mile in less than four minutes. Sports clubs in Germany have had strong political ties for more than a century and when Germans emigrated to the United States after 1848 they took *Turnen* with them and set up *Turnvereine*. The *Sozialistischer Turnerbund* founded in 1851 was certainly not without political significance when issues such as slavery became acute.

The connection between sport and military preparedness is sufficiently obvious to require but little attention in this introduction. A number of combat sports together with archery have grown out of military training. The tedium of the physical training which military training still involves can be endured only if an element of play is introduced. The Athenian sailors at the battle of Salamis, unlike the Persians, saved their lives when their ships were sunk because they were able to swim. Swimming was officially encouraged, so that a dunce was described as one who could neither write nor swim. In the twentieth century competitions and standard tests in hand-grenade-throwing have featured in the sports programme of more than one country, just as archery was practised as a paramilitary sport in towns and villages in medieval England. Even sports which have no direct military value, such as football, have been encouraged for their contribution to the physical fitness and physical courage which the fighting soldier needs in large measure to achieve victory. Government support for gliding in Germany during the 1930s, and perhaps the popularity of the sport, were due to a desire to evade the restrictive disarmament clauses of the Treaty of Versailles.

Sport, then touches human life at many points—so many that it is difficult to define the concept or set limits to sporting activity. *Idrott* in Sweden, *Spiel* in Germany, *athletics* in the United States admit precise definitions but the word *sport* has a much wider use than these. In origin French, it designates any diversion from the sad or serious side of life. It covers activities ranging from mountaineering to making love, from motor-racing to playing practical jokes. As a noun it can refer to a man, a woman, a game, a pastime, a chase, a hunt, a fight, a joke or even a botanical freak. The chapters that follow are not written as sociological study nor as history. They have been written rather as an extended essay upon some points where there has been, and still is, interaction between sport and the life and thought of man.

BIBLIOGRAPHY

FOR study of the anthropological background to sport the books listed here are suggested.

FRAZER, J. G., *The Golden Bough* (London, 1890), especially those volumes entitled "The Dying God" for a study of the origin of the Olympic Games. E. N. GARDINER in *Athletics of the Ancient World* (Oxford, 1931) gives alternative views to those in *The Golden Bough*.

LOVEJOY, A. O. and BOAS, G., *Primitivism and Related Ideas in Antiquity* (Baltimore, 1935).

LOWRIE, R. H., *The History of Ethnological Theory* (New York, 1937).

MALINOWSKI, B., *A Scientific Theory of Culture* (University of North Carolina, 1944).

MEAD, M., *Cooperation and Competition among Primitive Peoples* (Berkeley, University of California, 1946).

MUMFORD, L., *The City in History* (London, 1961).

SPENCE, L., *Myth and Ritual in Dance, Game and Rhyme* (London, 1947).

STUMPF, F. and COZENS, F. W., Some Aspects of the Role of Games, Sports and Recreational Activities in the Culture of Modern Primitive Peoples, *Research Quarterly*, **18**, 3, pp. 198–218 (Washington D.C., 1947).

PART I · YESTERDAY

II

THE OLYMPIC IDEAL AND ITS DOWNFALL

SPORT, despite its many ramifications, is so intimately associated with the human body and with bodily function and activity that different attitudes towards the body and the physical have inevitably affected, or been reflected in, attitudes to sport. Again, sport is essentially for leisure so that attitudes to leisure have likewise coloured attitudes to sport. These range through a scale of values. Some people believe that sport is its own justification, an end in itself, wherein man may express some of his highest and noblest aspirations. It has in it an element of worship and of sacrifice. Then there are those who hold that sport in itself is not particularly noble but is most valuable as a means to noble or at least desirable ends. At best sport may be an instrument of education for the training of character; it may provide harmless outlets for aggressive and socially harmful impulses; or it may be a therapeutic agent in the maintenance of physical health and fitness. Again, there are those who regard participation in sport as a concession to human frailty, a concession which some people may be able to avoid altogether. But for the mass of mankind, certainly in youth, sport is admitted to be an activity which can be pursued without damage to the personality or undue interference with labour or study. Indeed, the more serious business of life can be tackled with greater vigour after a respite devoted to sport. An extreme view of sport is that it is frivolous and even sinful so that it ought to be abjured by all serious and high-minded men and women. This attitude is often but not necessarily associated with certain religious beliefs on the nature of man and the conflict between mind and matter, though there have been professed agnostics who have adopted this extreme view.

These various ideas of sport and leisure have their adherents today; they are, however, not new and it may help to disentangle the web of modern sport if we examine first the attitudes of those who have gone before and especially the ideas of those who have shaped western European civilization. That sport in the days of Homeric heroes was noble there is no doubt. The funeral games of Patroclus and the Phaeacian games held in honour of Odysseus on his way home to Ithaca were heroic in concept and practice. Although the Phaeacian games were organized by King Alcinous for Odysseus he pleaded tiredness and a heavy heart as excuse for not taking part himself, but Laodamas taunted him with being a merchant, a tramp, and a money-grubber, lacking nobility of character and accomplishment. Odysseus, stung by his taunts, picked up the nearest discus, which was heavier than those of the other competitors, and lightly threw it far beyond the marks of the Phaeacians.

Homeric games were serious but not so serious that laughter was excluded. In the foot-race of Patroclus Odysseus enlisted the aid of the goddess Athene who caused Aias, then in the lead, to stumble and fall in some oxen's offal. He stood up and spitting out the filth said to the Argives: "Out on it, it was the goddess who spoiled my running, she who from of old like a mother standeth by Odysseus' side and helpeth him," but they all laughed happily at the sight of him.

In classical Greece the ideal of physical prowess appeared in sculpture and in poetry. Pindar's odes were composed for the most part during an upsurge of enthusiasm for athletics after the Persians had been defeated and driven back at the beginning of the fifth century B.C. His athletic victors were not activated by mercenary motives but by love of fame: "The shepherd and the ploughman and the fowler and he whom the sea feedeth strive to keep fierce famine from their bellies; but who so in the games or in war hath won delightful fame receiveth the highest rewards in fair words of citizens and of strangers."[1] The eleventh Olympian Ode epitomizes the nobility of the athlete. Strength and beauty are the gifts of Zeus, of the Graces and of Fate. But physical beauty must be matched by noble deeds. Natural gifts imply the duty of developing them and excellence can only be attained with God's help by "cost and toil."[2]

The Greek city states were individual in character and developed different political constitutions and ways of life. They were often in competition, and sometimes in open warfare with each other. They had combined forces to defeat the two Persian invasions launched upon Greece, by Darius in 490 B.C. and by Xerxes in 480 B.C. But after the decisive defeat of the Persians by sea at Salamis in 480 B.C. and on land at Plataea in 479 B.C. the Greek cities resumed their individual roles. Two power blocks developed, one led by Sparta and the other by Athens. They clashed in the disastrous Peloponnesian War which lasted with intervals of truce from 431 B.C. to 404 B.C. Yet the idea and the practice of Panhellenism were never lost. They were kept alive at three cultural centres that were respected by all Greeks alike in war and in peace. These centres were at Cos where the disciples of Hippocrates subjected health and disease to rational scrutiny, at Delphi where the oracle of Apollo drew inquiries from far and near, and at Olympia. To the last of these centres came competitors and spectators from all over the Greek world to meet under the protection of a sacred truce, whatever wars might rage. Although there were three other Panhellenic athletic festivals (at Nemea, the Nemean Festival; at Corinth, the Isthmian Festival; and at Delphi, the Pythian Festival) the Olympic Festival was pre-eminent among them as a centre for the expression of the human spirit through competitive sport. Whatever happened later to debase this and other athletic festivals in the formative period of the Games sport appeared self-justified. Moreover, the Olympic Festival brought together poets as well as athletes so that aesthetic, physical and spiritual effort were linked in one unity of expression.

A less idealistic and more utilitarian view of sport was taken in some cities and became more widely held during the fourth century B.C. Xenophon put into the mouth of Socrates a statement in favour of physical exercise as private preparation for war and as an aid to philosophy. "For even in that in which you think that there is least exercise of the body, namely thinking, who does not know that many fail greatly from ill health?" There is certainly a falling away from the positive and glorious ideal of athletic prowess expressed by Pindar when Socrates is made to say: "It is disgraceful for a person to grow old in self-neglect before he knows what he would become by rendering himself well formed and vigorous in body."

None took the utilitarian approach to sport further along the road to its logical conclusion than the Spartans. They depended for their very survival and for the survival of their polity upon the harsh and continuous suppression of a conquered people, the Helots. Annually war was formally declared upon the Helots and the Spartans orientated their whole way of life to military efficiency. They insisted that their sports coaches knew all about military tactics because they considered competitive sport as preliminary training for war. Even dancing, the most carefree of pastimes in peace, was directed to military training and we read that "the Spartans danced in such a way as though about to dodge a missile or to hurl one or to leap from the ground and to handle a shield skilfully."[3] But Sparta was atypical and earned the hearty condemnation of Aristotle: "While warfare was their means of self-preservation, the hegemony they achieved occasioned their decline, because they were ignorant of the use of leisure and had mastered no higher form of training than the art of war."[4]

Quite apart from the Spartan aberration the religious and cultural functions of the Olympic Games and of other Pan-hellenic festivals were obscured and then destroyed by specialization and commercialism. Popular heroes became pot hunters like Theagenes, winner of more than one thousand four hundred prizes in different festivals. By the end of the fifth century B.C. the appellation *athlete* was no longer a badge of honour but was the label of a special class who dieted and trained for their careers in such a way as to set them apart from ordinary citizens. Euripides thought that of all the myriad evils throughout Greece none was worse than the race of athletes. They neither learned how to live a good life nor could they do so.[5] Aristotle agreed that the athletes' habit of body neither produced good condition for the general purposes of civic life nor did it promote health and the pro-creation of children.[6] Euripides blamed the spectators for the decline of athletics and without doubt their adulation and the money which they brought to sport enabled valuable prizes to be offered and athletes to be remunerated as full-time specialist entertainers.

Success in the Games was sought for narrow political ends both by states and by individuals. The motives of the Athenian Alcibiades are well described by his son—

About the same time my father, seeing that the festival assembly at Olympia was beloved and admired by the whole world and that in it the Greeks made display of their wealth, strength of body and training, and that not only the athletes were the object of envy but that also the cities of the victors became renowned, and believing moreover that, while the public services performed in Athens redound to the prestige, in the eyes of his fellow citizens, of the person who renders them, expenditures in the Olympic Festivals, however, enhance the city's reputation throughout Greece; reflecting on these things, I say . . . he entered a larger number of teams in competition than even the mightiest cities had done, and they were of such excellence that he came out first, second and third . . . And when he brought his mission to an end he had caused the successes of his predecessors to seem petty in comparison with his own and those who in his day had been victors to be no longer objects of emulation.[7]

When the Romans pacified and organized the whole Mediterranean world they permitted and encouraged the sports of the stadium and the hippodrome—not now the pursuits of free-born citizens destined for power and influence in their states, but the competitions of members of a specialized profession with their unions, coaches, training schools, and their conditions of service accepted and approved by the Emperor himself. At the same time life in the cities of the empire and especially in Rome developed in such a way that "keeping fit" became a major problem for many people.

For the mass of the population in Rome, about a million and a quarter during the second and third centuries A.D., the facilities for physical recreation were more elaborate than they had ever been before or have been since. For the most part the facilities were to be found within the Thermae or Baths. For instance, the Baths of Trajan, measuring two hundred and eighty by two hundred and ten metres, included hot rooms, cold rooms, and a swimming bath, two *palaestrae* for general exercise and a running-track. The perimeter buildings contained as well as a library, administrative offices and refreshment rooms, gymnasia and courts for ball-games. This was a large establishment and like the baths of Nero, of Caracalla, and of Diocletian, had been provided by an anxious despotism to placate a politically powerless population and to provide outlets for energies which might otherwise have become too dangerous for the safety of the prince and the stability of his government.

By the fourth century A.D. there were eight hundred and fifty-six baths great and small in Rome and it would have been possible for upwards of sixty thousand people to be using them at the same time either free of charge or for a nominal sum. Within their walls sport had become either a gentle pastime or a form of therapy assisted by a corps of masseurs and trainers. The Stoic philosopher Seneca who had lodgings near one of these establishments described a typical scene in a bath. There was a man doing weight-training, another, less active, having a cheap rub down, some others playing a ball game with a *pilicrepus*, some kind of attendant, to call out the score, a noisy man singing in his bath and another making an unconscionable noise and splashing in the swimming pool. Sport here was not very elevated but even Seneca, who despised the cult of the body on the ground that however strong your sinews were you could never be a match for a first-class bull, nevertheless recommended to his readers such activities as running, weight training, high and long jumping and certain forms of dance and, indeed, any "short and simple exercises which tire the body rapidly and so save time."

The reduction of sport to therapeutic exercise is seen most clearly in the works of Galen who was physician to the emperor Commodus and died in the year A.D. 201. Of three works concerned with physical activity, two of them, *On Health* and *Whether Health is the Concern of Medicine or Gymnastics*, are so intimately concerned with therapeutic exercise that they are hardly relevant to sport. The third work on *Exercises with the Small Ball* inevitably touches on games and sport. It is significant that Galen found it necessary to say at the outset: 'The best gymnastics is that which not only exercises the body but delights the spirit. This is especially true of small ball gymnastics.' Neither Plato nor Aristotle who had vigorously pleaded the cause of gymnastics in their general system of education felt it necessary to make any appeal to enjoyment. In their day gymnastics had consisted on the one hand of activities which made an immediate appeal as competitive events—running, wrestling, throwing the discus, and on the other it embraced forms of training which were necessary to survival in warfare.

Five hundred years later the urban life of Rome had sapped the physical vigour of her citizens. It had done more than this. The provision of food and entertainment in theatre, amphitheatre and circus, at no cost in effort or money to the ordinary man, had undermined the very desire to strive and strain and to exercise physical skill in co-operation or in competition with others. It is true that many of the activities of the Greek *palaestrae* and gymnasia could have been seen at the baths in Rome or on the eight *campi* used by the multitude, as Strabo notes, for "ball-playing, hoop trundling or wrestling," but they lacked the motive power which the Panhellenic and local games had given to sport in the Greek city state. Galen was hard put to it to devise activities—pseudo sports—which men would enjoy doing to maintain basic physical fitness.

The problem of keeping fit in Rome was aggravated by the growth in the total amount of leisure, the consequent decrease of casual exercise involved in daily work and the development of the habit of watching rather than doing. As early as the reign of Claudius in the first century A.D. one hundred and fifty-nine days were marked as public holidays of which as many as ninety-three might be devoted to "games" at public expense. By A.D. 354 there were two hundred public holidays and one hundred and seventy-five days of "games." More than half the year was leisure and even on working days, work which began at daybreak would cease soon after noon during much of the year. Neither the five-day nor the forty-hour week has yet given to the modern worker the leisure that the inhabitants of Rome had to fill.

The public spectacles which played so large a part in the life of Rome were partly sporting and partly theatrical. Chariot-racing in the hippodrome was one of the more innocent shows, and the Circus Maximus might accommodate 385,000 spectators. At the theatre of Marcellus, which held some fifty thousand spectators, lewd and violent shows were staged, while at the Amphitheatre animals and human beings were maimed and butchered in a variety of cruel and ingenious ways before a holiday crowd of fifty thousand. It seems that almost half the population of Rome could be accommodated simultaneously in its circuses, theatres and amphitheatres. Even Pompeii had an amphitheatre holding twenty thousand people—more than half the adult population. After the decay of Rome, watching on this scale only became possible once more when television was invented.

The denial of any value at all to sport and efforts to reduce physical activity and function to the bare necessities of existence have been features of certain religious and philosophical systems from prehistoric times onwards. Physical austerity and abstinence were practised in Africa, Oceania and by the early Indians of the Americas. They are also to be found in the oriental religious Buddhism, Hinduism, Sikhism and Shintoism. For our study, however, interest centres upon the changes of Greek thought upon physical activity and physical prowess and in particular upon the development of asceticism in the Roman world.

Plato's and Aristotle's views on leisure (σχόλη) provide a

starting-point. For Plato the philosopher is the man of leisure who is free to follow the argument wherever it may lead him. There is no law restraining him and he is certainly not restricted nor debased by being forced to earn a living by trade or craft. The fact that rowing is included in the list of ignoble and debasing occupations merely underlines the view that physical activity can become ennobling only when it is severed from gainful occupation and is an end in itself, when, in fact, it becomes sport for sport's sake. The freedom of the philosopher has a spiritual significance. The education of the philosopher and of the guardian of the ideal state is fully dealt with in *The Republic*; "music" and "gymnastics" are its twin parts. The word used for this physical training in Plato's theory of education is ascesis (ἄσκησις). The words *athletic* and *ascetic* were in some senses interchangeable. All the same, Plato was not satisfied with current athletic training which had already in his time (427–347 B.C.) begun to be specialized. In his view it seemed to produce a sleepy habit and a health that was easily upset. "We need," he said, "a finer sort of training (ἄσκησις) for our champions." This would involve attention to diet, temperance in drinking coupled with hard endurance training and exercise. The purpose of bodily training was to enable man as a whole to reach and fulfil his highest functions.[8] In his later works Plato showed signs of being less interested in physical performance and prowess. "Human affairs are not worth serious attention, yet we take them seriously. Unfortunately for us we cannot help it. Only God is to be taken seriously."[9]

Aristotle had a more empirical approach to philosophy and to life than Plato. His tests for the success of political institutions rested on stability and contentment rather than on virtue. Yet he was in agreement with Plato on equating freedom with nobility. Leisure and leisure-time activities are the highest goods—

It is true that citizens of our state must be able to lead a life of action and war; but they must be even more able to lead a life of leisure and peace. It is true, again, that they must be able to do necessary or useful acts; but they must be even more able to do good acts. These are the general aims which ought to be followed in the education of childhood and of the stages of adolescence which still require education.[10]

Physical education was to precede education of the mind. Children were not to be made vulgar (βάναυσος) and any work or craft was vulgar which made men unfit for the exercise of virtue, but even liberal pursuits could become illiberal if carried to excess. It is for this reason that Aristotle condemns the way of life of the athlete: "The best habit is that which comes midway between the athletic and the valetudinarian—the exertion must not be violent or specialized, as is the case with the athlete; it should rather be a general exertion directed to all the activities of a free man."[11] Gymnastics which offered training in courage and the exercise of that virtue was conducive to the highest good. Courage demanded by mountaineering or by competitive sport when endurance is tested to the limit would seem to be fully in accordance with Aristotle's ideal of leisure. On the other hand play (παίδια) and recreation (ἀνάπαυσις) were not to be confused with leisure. They were rather related by him to un-leisure and were identified as curatives for the stress and pain which were implicit in the lack of leisure. As with Plato it is the quality of the physical activity or the sport which ennobles rather than the performance of movements, exercises or skills. In Aristotle's writings, as in Plato's, the word ascesis (ἄσκησις) is used for training.

How then did this word change its meaning? Before the advent of Christianity the Cynic and Stoic philosophers had already exalted the power of the human will to such an enormous extent that the body and bodily training were at first subordinated to the mind and then came to be despised as such. The specialized and socially useless training of the athlete gave some encouragement to this process. To Diogenes the cynic are attributed significant antics at the Isthmian Games. When asked whether he had come as a spectator he said: "No, but to compete in them myself." The man with a laugh asked who his competitors were. "Hardships", replied Diogenes, "which are very difficult and unconquerable by men stuffed with food and dazed ... I really think these athletes have less intelligence than swine."[12] He subsequently placed a crown on the head of a horse which had, so he said, been victorious over another horse in a kicking match.

Already before the birth of Christ Greek philosophers had begun to revolt against the physical excesses of athletic festivals and they thought of training (ἄσκησις) no longer as leading to a supreme physical achievement in sport but as a means to subordinating the body for spiritual ends. In Palestine the Essene sect also developed a community life with a similar end in view.

By the time of the Emperor Tiberius A.D. 14–37 competitive sport in the Roman Empire had been commercialized and professionalized. Combat sports in particular had been debased into displays of cruelty in which gladiators fought to the death for the entertainment of mass audiences. The more innocent sports of running, throwing and jumping were organized under guilds or unions of professional performers so that sport, on its higher levels of skill, was entertainment and was often identifiable with it in a debased form. Competitive sport, then, no longer manifested the ideal of physical prowess which in earlier days had seemed a worthy end of training or asceticism.

The word asceticism occurs once only in the New Testament, when Paul is defending himself before Felix and says "and herein do I exercise myself (ἀσκῶ) to have always a conscience void of offence toward God and toward men" (Acts XXIV, 16). In the First Epistle to the Corinthians (IX, 15) the Christian life is compared with the Games in which "every man that striveth for the mastery is temperate in all things: now they do it to obtain a corruptible crown but we are incorruptible. I therefore so run, not as uncertainly; so fight I not as one that beateth the air; but I keep under my body and bring it into subjection" (δουλαγωγῶ). The idea of enslaving the body is in strong contrast with Platonic and Aristotelian ideas of training for freedom.

For some years the earlier concept of training persisted alongside a new one. Clemens of Alexandria at the end of the second century strongly recommended games and athletics for boys and men and at the same time represented the Christian life as ascesis and the patriarch Jacob as an ascetic. Later, however, the negative aspect of asceticism received more emphasis. Jerome developed the concept from one of general endurance to that of suffering in prison, earnestness in prayer and self-chosen poverty and abstention from marriage.

Such abstention was a form of self-denial which came to have a particular association with asceticism. There developed also among early Christians especially in Egypt an increasing respect for austerites and a belief in the inherent pollution of the world. In the third century A.D. many Egyptian Christians adopted a way of life not merely strict and austere, but one which estranged them from all earthly ties which could be severed. They often resorted to the wilderness to achieve this end. Soon this ascetic life became a corporate way of life. Pachamius was the first to form a community of ascetics in the fourth century and from this time *ascetic* in its specialized sense was nearly equivalent to *monastic*.

The extreme perversion of the asceticism of Plato and Aristotle by early Christians is recorded by Sozomen and reproduced by Gibbon[13]—

C

It was the practice of the monks either to cut or shave their hair; they wrapped their heads in a cowl, to escape the sight of profane objects ... The aspects of a genuine Anchoret was horrid and disgusting; every sensation that is offensive to men was thought acceptable to God; and the angelic rule of Tabenne condemned the salutary custom of bathing the limbs in water and of anointing them with oil ...

They sunk under their painful weights of crosses and chains; and their emaciated limbs were confirmed by collars, bracelets, gauntlets and greaves of massy and rigid iron. All superfluous incumbrance of dress was contemptuously cast away; and some savage saints of both sexes have been admired whose naked bodies were only covered by their long hair. They aspired to reduce themselves to the rude and miserable state in which the human brute is scarcely distinguished above his kindred animals; and the numerous sect of Anchorets derived their name from their humble practice of grazing in the fields of Mesopotamia with the common herd.

Many fanatic exponents of asceticism have been condemned by the Roman Catholic Church and among them have been the Gnostics, the Manichees and the Albigenses. Nevertheless asceticism has persisted in strength both inside and outside the Church of Rome, and the term whether in its general or in its special sense equivalent to monasticism, looks back to the theology and practice of early Christians, not to the concepts of Plato and Aristotle. As a protest against the commercial athleticism and paganism of the ancient world it was effective, but from the time when the Christian emperor Theodosius II launched his vigorous anti-pagan campaign in 408, to which the Olympic and other festivals fell victims, asceticism has always been inimical to the ennoblement and even to the toleration of sport.

BIBLIOGRAPHY

1. PINDAR, *Odes* I, 1 (trans. Ernest Myers, pp. 47 *et seq.*).
2. PINDAR, *Odes* I 1, 42; 4, 57; 5, 10.
3. PHILOSTRATUS, *On Gymnastics*, ch. 19.
4. ARISTOTLE, *Politics*, II.
5. EURIPIDES, Autolycus, fragment 282. in *Trag. Graec. Frag.*, ed. Nauck, trans. W. A. Oldfather.
6. ARISTOTLE, *Politics*, VII, 16, 12.
7. ISOCRATES, *Team of Horses*, 32–34.
8. PLATO, *Republic*, 403E–404B.
9. PLATO, *Laws*, 803B.
10. ARISTOTLE, *Politics*, VII, 14, 12–15.
11. ARISTOTLE, *Politics*, VII, 13.
12. DIO CHRYSOSTOM, Oration, VII, II.
13. GIBBON E., *Decline and Fall of the Roman Empire*, Chap. XXXVII.

See also

CARCOPINO, J., *Daily Life in Ancient Rome* (London, 1941).
GARDINER, E. N., *Athletics of the Ancient World* (Oxford, 1931).
GIBBON, E., *Decline and Fall of the Roman Empire* (*passim*).
MCINTOSH, P. C., DIXON, J. G., MUNROW, A. D., and WILLETTS, R. F., *Landmarks in the History of Physical Education* (London, 1957).
ROBINSON, R. S., *Sources for the History of Greek Athletics* (pub. the author, 338 Probasco Street, Cincinnati 20, Ohio).
Oxford Dictionary of the Christian Church, Ascetism.

III

MEDIEVAL INTERLUDE

BETWEEN the accession of Theodosius in A.D. 408 and the Renaissance of classical learning and of humanism in Italy in the fourteenth century there elapsed nearly a thousand years. The period is not well documented for the historian, especially not for the historian of sport. The theories of Plato and Aristotle were not unknown. In the thirteenth century there was an Aristotelian Renaissance when the Schoolmen and St. Thomas Aquinas in particular brought the *Politics* of Aristotle back into the general current of European political thought. Yet social and economic conditions in Europe were so different from the *polis* in which Aristotle wrote and even from the *cosmopolis* of Alexander the Great which succeeded it that it is hardly surprising if sporting practices were very different from those which Aristotle knew or advocated. Moreover, it was in the monasteries and through the celibate ecclesiastical orders that the philosophy of the ancient world was handed on. With few exceptions their interpretation of physical training or "ascesis" was radically different from that of Aristotle, even if on occasions in practice their asceticism was relaxed in favour of the pleasures of life —even sport. Against Chaucer's hunting monk who—

> . . . yaf nat of that text a pulled hen,
> That seith, that hunters been not holy men.

must be set many who, like Abailard, were able to persuade themselves that sickness of the body was good for mental progress.

Notwithstanding asceticism the so-called Dark Ages and the medieval period which succeeded them had a wealth of sports and pastimes. Many sports in current practice in the nineteenth and twentieth centuries existed in a rudimentary form during the Middle Ages. Attempts are often made to trace the lineal descent of modern games even further back to Roman, Greek or even Egyptian origins. The origin of football, for instance, is sometimes attributed to the Roman game of *harpastum* or the Greek game *episcyros*, but no continuous line of development can be traced with any certainty. On the contrary, forms of football have been found in many parts of the world in communities unconnected with each other. In China "the emperor Ch'eng Ti (36–32 B.C.) was fond of football; but his officers represented to him that it was both physically exhausting and also unsuitable to the imperial dignity. His Majesty replied "We like playing and what one chooses to do is not exhausting." An appeal being made to the Empress she suggested tiddliwinks for the Emperor's amusement."[1] More recently in the New Hebrides the natives played a game of football using a coco-nut or bread-fruit for a ball and two live pigs as goals. It is not possible to establish any historical association between these and many other forms of football that have been recorded. Football is a game that has erupted many times in human history. The same may be said of other sports.

Moreover, in looking back to the life of the ancient world it is clear that the destruction of the stadia, the amphitheatres and, above all, the baths of the Roman world inevitably led to the decline and disappearance of sports and techniques of sports which had been elaborated. The pattern of sport in the Middle Ages was almost entirely discontinuous with that of the ancient world. It is the more interesting, therefore, to find certain features of the pattern which are comparable with those of an earlier period.

Joseph Strutt who, in 1801, wrote his comprehensive survey of British sport "from the earliest period to the present time," classified sports under three broad headings: "rural exercises practised by persons of rank," "rural exercises generally practised" and "pastimes usually exercised in towns and cities, or places adjoining to them." He was perhaps imposing upon the past those geographical and social distinctions which he drew from observation of the society at the end of the eighteenth century. Nevertheless he found it possible without distorting his evidence to notice in the sports of the Middle Ages these fundamental distinctions between rural and urban and between aristocratic and plebeian.

The rise and decline of the tournament illustrates the latter distinction particularly well. Tournaments and jousting were introduced to England by the Norman nobility. The tournament was a martial conflict in which great numbers of knights engaged. In early days it was certainly a violent exercise and earned the condemnation of the Church and, from time to time, prohibition by statute. At times it was realistic military training and not sport at all. Even when, in the thirteenth century, the tournament was becoming to some extent formalized it was still a war game of considerable military value. While the tournament was a contest between teams, a joust was a trial of skill between two individual knights. The combats took place upon horseback and the knights and esquires were attended by pages who rendered services to them during the contests. The object of both sports was to unhorse the opponent. At first the combatants in a tournament stationed themselves at four corners of an open place and ran against each other at will. Then cords were stretched in front of the companies who might not advance until the heralds withdrew or cut the cords. Then from France came the "double lists" where the knights might run from one side or the other without coming into contact except with their lances. An elaborate code of laws and regulations was drawn up for the preliminary arrangements and for the combat itself.

There were also cruder and less formal forms of jousting and tilting practised by those who could not aspire to knighthood or claim the title of esquire, but the tournament and jousting, according to Strutt, were prohibited to all below the rank of an esquire.

In the age of chivalry the mere management of arms, although essentially requisite, was not sufficient of itself to form an accomplished knight. Specialization in sport was deplored by the nobility. To be skilled in music, to dance gracefully, to ride well, were also required of a knight as well as urbanity of manners and physical courage. The development of this concept required wealth, leisure, and peace, at least, for considerable intervals of time and Strutt remarks that "the romantic notions of chivalry appear to have lost their vigour towards the conclusion of the fifteenth century, especially in this country where a continued series of intestine commotions employed the exertions of every man of property, and real battles afforded but little leisure to exercise the mockery of war."

While the tournament was from time to time suppressed by statute, the sport of archery was positively encouraged especially by Edward III, Richard II and Edward IV, so important was this skill for military purposes. Every Englishman and Irishman dwelling in England was commanded to have a bow his own height, butts were to be made in every town and the inhabitants were to shoot on all feast days under penalty of a halfpenny fine for every omission. Furthermore, useless and idle pursuits such as football were forbidden in some cities including London, because they drew men away from the more useful sport of archery. There was nothing exclusive about archery; it was for all and sundry.

Hunting and the taking of wild animals for food or for pleasure had from Saxon times been notable pastimes. Moreover, the sport of hunting had been sharply divided into rich men's and poor men's sports. The king himself designated certain areas royal forests of which the most famous is the New Forest in Hampshire designated by William of Normandy. The protection of these forests for the sport of the king and of those to whom he was pleased to grant a similar privilege was enforced by officers appointed in every country and shire to enforce rigorous Game Laws. The Forest Charter of King John did insist that no man should forfeit his life or his limbs for killing the king's deer, but if he was taken in the act of stealing the king's venison he should be subjected to a heavy fine, and in default of payment to imprisonment for a year and a day and then to banishment unless he could produce a surety for good behaviour.

Hunting seems to have been favoured by the clergy. Arch-bishops, bishops, earls and barons were given permission by King John to take one or two deer when travelling through royal forests. This was later construed as a general permission for people of these ranks to hunt in royal chases. The evidence for hunting by the clergy is extensive, much of it appearing as reproaches by poets and other writers. Chaucer severely re-proached priests in the "Ploughman's Tale" because they thought more of hunting with their dogs and blowing the horn than of the service which they owed to God. Henry II, while not withdrawing from the upper clergy the privilege to hunt in royal forests, endeavoured to enforce the canon law which forbade the clergy to spend time in hunting and hawking and he obtained authority from the Papal legate to bring offenders before secular courts. Nevertheless, bishops and abbots of the Middle Ages hunted with great state. Thomas à Becket being sent by Henry II as ambassador to the court of France took with him dogs and hawks of various sorts such as were used by kings and princes. At the time of the Reforma-tion the see of Norwich possessed thirteen parks stocked with deer and other animals for the chase.

Sport as a public spectacle which had been so highly developed in the Roman world and all too often had taken the
form of elaborately devised cruelty to beast and man died
away with the decline of the Roman Empire. Sport as a
spectacle in one form or another may never have completely
disappeared. It seemed to meet a demand which was basic
within an urban community. There might not always have
been well-built amphitheatres, stadia or theatres but there
were always courts and common or open land where men
and women could gather to watch feats of skill or daring or
strength. Fitzstephen describing life in London in the twelfth
century wrote that every year on Shrove Tuesday boys in-
dulged in cock-fighting in the morning while "after dinner,
all the youths go into the fields to play ball. The scholars of
every school have their ball or baston in their hands; the
ancient and wealthy men of the city come forth on horseback
to see the sport of the young men and to take part of the
pleasure in beholding their agility." Again in the Easter
holidays water jousting from boats on the Thames was
organized and then "upon the bridge, wharfs and houses by
the river's side, stand great numbers to see and laugh there at."
A number of sporting spectacles exhibited cruelty, not in
the form of bloody massacres of men specially prepared for
that fate, but in the form of animal-baiting. The training of
bulls, bears and even horses for baiting by dogs was regularly
undertaken by "jugglers," that is professional entertainers.
Boars too were used to fight each other for the amusement of
the public. Several places in London were specifically set aside
for animal-baiting. The Paris Garden in Southwark contained
two beargardens. "Those who go to Paris Garden, the Bell
Savage or Theatre, to behold bear-baiting, enterludes or fence
play, must not account of any pleasant spectacle unless first
they pay one pennie at the gate, another at the entry of the
scaffold and a third for quiet standing."[2] Commercialized

cruelty has frequently appeared in civilized societies and even in our own day is ready to jump forward. Bullfighting is, of course, well established in Spain and the cruelty cannot be and is not disguised. Animal-baiting is strictly forbidden by law but hunting fox and stag have earned for themselves the name "blood sports," and whatever useful functions they perform and whatever innocent and healthy pleasure they give, the underlying appeal is to human traits which are associated with cruelty. Even boxing as a spectacle, hedged around as it is with regulations and medical precautions, excites in the audience emotions which batten on the infliction of pain and the drawing of blood so that accounts of fights, even when they appear in the most reputable papers, dwell upon the opening up of a cut over the eye or upon some other painful feature of the combat.

Sport in the Middle Ages was often cruel and violent. With few exceptions it was more spontaneous and less highly organized than in modern times. Yet many of our modern sports had medieval ancestors or medieval variants and in town and country sport and play were prominent features of leisure for rich and poor.

BIBLIOGRAPHY

1. GILES, M.A., 'Football in China' in *Nineteenth Century* (March, 1906).
2. STRUTT, J., *The Sports and Pastimes of the People of England*, III, 6, 17 (London, 1903).

See also

DUKE OF BEAUFORT *et al.*, Eds., *Badminton Library of Sports and Pastimes* (London, 1886 *et seq.*)

COULTON, G. G., *The Medieval Scene* (Cambridge, 1930).

COULTON, G. G., *Medieval Panorama* (Cambridge, 1938).

GREEN, J. R., *A Short History of the English People* (London, 1895).

EARL OF LONSDALE *et al.* Eds., *Lonsdale Library of Sports, Games and Pastimes* (London, 1929).

TREVELYAN, G. M., *English Social History* (London, 1944).

WYMER, N., *Sport in England* (London, 1949).

IV

THE PURITANS AND SPORT

SPORT in the Middle Ages had been widespread and it reflected the structure of society. The Renaissance of learning which began in Italy in the fourteenth century and spread throughout Europe was associated with and was dependent upon a different social and economic structure. In England in 1265 Simon de Montfort had summoned two citizens from every borough to sit beside two knights from every county with the barons and ecclesiastics in Parliament at Westminster. The invitation was symptomatic of the growing importance of the towns and townsmen. This trend was not confined to England but was to be seen throughout western Europe. In Italy the growth of towns and small states enjoying prosperity and using a money economy was advanced by the fifteenth century. In these states there emerged a new class of property and intellect, so new that Aeneas Sylvius (later Pope Pius II) was able to write in the fifteenth century: "In our change-loving Italy, where nothing stands firm, and where no ancient dynasty exists, a servant can easily become a king." Inevitably the idea that nobility depended upon birth gave ground but the concept of nobility and of a noble class remained. The distinction too between noble and ignoble in sport also remained although it took on a new guise.

The revival of learning and the emergence of new political and social organization did not come as a sudden break with the past, and sports of the nobility in the age of chivalry continued to attract the new nobility in Italy. Tournaments in particular, now formalized more than ever, were popular. Burckhardt in his *Civilization of the Renaissance in Italy* wrote

35

that "it was in vain that from the time of Petrarch downwards the tournament was denounced as a dangerous folly. No one was convinced by the pathetic appeal of the poet: 'In what book do we read that Scipio or Caesar were skilled at the joust?' The practice became more and more popular in Florence. Every honest citizen came to consider his tournament—now no doubt less dangerous than formerly—as fashionable sport ... It may be mentioned that a passionate interest in this sport was displayed by the Medici as if they wished to show, private citizens as they were, without noble blood in their veins, that the society which surrounded them was in no respect inferior to a Court."[1]

A new sport which the Italian nobility developed for their enjoyment was football, highly organized under the title *calcio*. As in the tournament rival pavilions were set up, there were elaborate preliminaries and rival teams wore fine and colourful costumes. The technique of the game was highly developed but the point of interest here is the social exclusiveness of the game. In Florence regulations stipulated: "Moreover, even as every kind of man was not admitted to the Olympic Games, but only men of standing in their native cities and kingdoms, so, in the *calcio*, all kinds of rascallions are not to be tolerated, neither artificers, servants nor lowborn fellows, but honourable soldiers, gentlemen, lords and princes."[2] When in the nineteenth century the Henley Regatta Committee and the Amateur Athletic Club decided to define the term amateur to exclude anyone who was "by trade or employment a mechanic, artisan or labourer" they were translating into a contemporary idiom a traditional feature of sport. In similar vein Castiglione, that great authority on the life and accomplishments of a courtier, in 1528 had commended "tenyse" and "vautynge" which, he said, made a man lighter and quicker than anything else but condemned tumbling and rope-climbing as fit only for jugglers.

Noble patronage of a sport resulted not merely in technical development but also in conventions and taboos which were observed more carefully perhaps than the rules themselves. In fourteenth-century England, physical prowess by itself had not had the stamp of nobility. It must exhibit also the qualities of "loyautie" and of "courtaysie."[3] In fifteenth-century Italy the idea of "courtesy" was developed further so that prowess in sport was to be accompanied by *gratia*. Indeed, the truly noble person must take such pains to avoid ostentation of his ability that he often concealed it. This ideal of behaviour was not confined to Italy, and the opening scenes of *As You Like It* contained a wrestling incident which exmplified this facet of sport. Charles, the Duke's professional wrestler whose prowess was well known, was matched against Orlando, the dispossessed son of a noble father. Orlando was not expected to win. In fact that match had been engineered by his brother for the express purpose of dispatching the brother whom he had ousted from his inheritance. Orlando, however, overthrew the professional with deceptive ease. So in Italy it was required of a courtier that he perform his skills with *sprezzatura* (disdain), and physical virtuosity, once attained, was to be revealed rather than exhibited.

In fourteenth-century Italy, as in the age of chivalry and in classical Greece, the concept of nobility, while it included physical prowess in sport as an essential element, nevertheless was subject to the danger of specialization of the personality in physical activity. Prowess in any physical activity had to be kept in perspective, and specific injunctions are given by teachers and writers decrying this specialization, especially in the profession of arms.

The fifteenth century in Italy was a time of interstate feuds and wars. Not even the employment of mercenary troops relieved the nobleman of the need to be fit for military campaigns. Some sports, therefore, were fostered and encouraged for their military value. Hunting, running, leaping, swimming and casting the barre were advocated by Castiglione as being "not directly dependent on arms but being akin to them."

Economic and political conditions such as those which allowed a class of property and intellect in Italy to develop a characteristic pattern of sport did not exist in England until after the victory of Henry Tudor at Bosworth Field and his accession to the throne as Henry VII. The traditional date for the end of the Middle Ages, 1485, did not appear to those who were alive at the time to be a year profoundly different from other years. As in Italy, medieval sports like the tournament continued in vogue but during the sixteenth century there was a new surge forward for the nobility and the gentry led by the king. Henry VIII in his younger days was a vigorous and skilled athlete who participated in wrestling, fencing, running and throwing events and ball-games, as well as in hunting and horsemanship. He is reported to have had wrestling bouts with Francis I, King of France, which he did not win; he laid down bowling alleys at Whitehall and he constructed the Tennis Court at Hampton Court in 1529. Italian coaches for sports were much in vogue. Henry VIII introduced to his court as his riding master Robert Alexander who had studied the Italian art of training the horse described by Grisone, Fiaschi and Caracciole and who had been a pupil of the Neopolitan master Pignatelli. In fencing, too, Italian masters were in demand. The professors of the art were incorporated by Letters Patent of July 1540 by Henry VIII to teach the Noble Science of Defence in which scholars took degrees and proceeded to be Provosts of Defence.

The court was undoubtedly at the forefront of the Tudor sports movement, but in town and country the nobility and gentry fostered and avidly practised old and new sports. The attempt was made to restrict noble sports to the nobility but in a time of affluence sports had a way of crossing social boundaries. In 1535 Henry had forbidden tennis, among other games, on pain of a fine of twenty shillings to all persons other than noblemen and property-owners, yet in 1558 a visiting French ecclesiastic, Maistre Étienne Perlin, wrote: "Whilst I remained in England, there were garrisons all over the country. The people make good cheer, and dearly love junketing; and you will see many rich taverns, and the tavern-keepers have commonly large purses, in which are one, three or four smaller ones, full of money; whence you may gather that this country is very rich, and that people in trade gain more in one week than those in Germany or Spain do in a month; for here you may commonly see artisans such as hatters and joiners, playing at tennis for a crown, which is not often seen elsewhere particularly on a working day."[4]

Cock-fighting was a sport which was practised and watched by all and sundry, so too was archery. Henry VIII had built a royal cockpit in St. James's Fields (Birdcage Walk) which survived until 1816. Archery, however, in spite of the encouragement and the personal example of both Henry VIII and Elizabeth I and in spite of the apology of Roger Ascham in his book *Toxophilus* suffered some decline in Tudor England. Competition from other attractive sports and the diminishing relevance of the use of the bow in warfare lowered participation in the sport of archery.

If a number of noble sports spread downwards through social classes there were some popular games which never spread upwards. Football was one of these. As played in streets and open spaces the game was violent and dangerous, devoid of grace and skill. The game was strictly forbidden, but was obviously played, nevertheless, at Oxford and Cambridge. It came under interdiction at Cambridge in 1574 and at Oxford in 1584 when any minister or deacon convicted of playing football was to be banished and reported to his bishop; scholars over eighteen were to be imprisoned and fined, and those under eighteen were to be flogged in St. Mary's Church. "Beastly fury and extreme violence leaving rancour and malice behind," was Sir Thomas Elyot's description of the game. Philip Stubbes in his *Anatomy of Abuses* protested that it might "rather be called a friendly kind of fight than play or recreation; a bloody and murthering practise than a fellowly sport or pastime"—and this, in most places, it remained until it was refined and organized by the gentry of the nineteenth century. Tudor gentry would have none of it.

Elizabeth I was the child of her father and of her age in that she was an accomplished performer with the bow and in dancing and enjoyed watching games and sports on her peregrinations about the realm. Sports and junketings were a feature of English life, and allusions to them abound in Shakespeare's plays. The solitary allusion to football merely confirms the disrepute of that game. In a scene when Lear and Kent are abusing Oswald the final slur is when Kent trips him up and calls him "a base football player."

And what of asceticism during the Renaissance? It is clear that many of those who were prominent in the new world of sport were devout in their religion. Neither the Italian princes nor the Tudor court in England was irreligious, yet it was at court rather than in the universities or in the schools which were founded in response to the new enthusiasm for classical learning that sport flourished. In England Erasmus did more than anyone to teach and preach the new humanism, yet he was no particular friend of sport and had little use for it and his admiration for Greek did not extend to admiration for Pindar or adoption of Plato's or Aristotle's views on gymnastics and asceticism. While a monk at a monastery in Steyn he wrote an essay "On the Contempt of the World" in which, in an unplatonic way, he sets the body in antagonism to the soul.

"The monks," he said, "do not choose to become like

cattle; they know that there is something sublime and divine within man whch they prefer to develop rather than to cater for the body. Man's nature is more dignified than that of the beast. Our body, except for a few details, differs not from an animal's body but our soul reaches out after things divine and eternal. The body is earthly, wild, slow, mortal, diseased, ignoble; the soul on the other hand is heavenly, subtle, divine, immortal, noble. Who is so blind that he cannot tell the difference between body and soul? And so the happiness of the soul surpasses that of the body."[5] Although Erasmus later came to despise many features of scholasticism and of the monasteries where it was practised yet he never found a very important or dignified place for physical activity in his philosophical or educational thinking. Children above the age of six were not to have physical education. In his *Colloquies* when the boys ask for a holiday for games the master replies, "they that labour hard had need of some relaxation; but you that study idly and play laboriously had more need of a curb than a snaffle." It is hardly surprising that St. Paul's and other schools founded under the inspiration of Erasmus found no place for sport other than as a concession to human frailty. Merchant Taylors' School under an enlightened headmaster, Richard Mulcaster, was an honourable exception but practices there do not seem to have been followed elsewhere.

The dissolution of the orders of monks and friars in the reign of Henry VIII was a natural outcome of the attitude towards religion and life in general which Erasmus, Colet, and his other friends and disciples had encouraged. Whatever Erasmus may have thought of sport the ascetic ideal which had been handed on in the monasteries ever since their foundation in the fourth century was no longer admired nor indeed was it practised at all assiduously by the monks.

It might be thought that the pejorative view of sport and the pleasures of sport might have perished both in England with the dissolution of the monasteries and in those parts of Europe where the teaching of Luther and Calvin prevailed. But the Reformation had within it the seeds of a new asceticism. It is true that the doctrine of justification by faith undermined the basis of monasticism and asceticism as it was then practised. Luther himself when he broke away from the monastic life, found an important place for physical education and believed that the civil authorities should give their citizens physical training as they already gave them military training. "Accordingly I pronounce in favour of ... the knightly sports of fencing and wrestling of which the one drives care and gloom from the heart and the other gives a full development to the limbs." Luther, Zwingli and Commenius all wanted the sports of the nobility extended to the people at large if only because of the other benefits which physical training in them would bring. In Geneva Calvin, although he had no use for ascetic monasticism, yet in his attempt to perfect moral discipline was led to curb all normal amusements. Calvin himself went for walks and played quoits until his old age, saying: "As I see that we cannot forbid men all diversions, I confine myself to those that are really bad" and named dicing and dancing as crimes. In the bylaws for his academy at Geneva he recommended a period of recreation on Wednesdays "but in such a way that all silly sports be avoided." Calvinsim was imported into England and there in its Puritan form it proved a greater enemy to sport than monasticism had been. Its influence grew during the reign of Elizabeth; Trevelyan has pointed out that, when the Queen succeeded her sister Mary, Puritanism was mainly a foreign doctrine imported from Geneva and the Rhineland; when she died it was rootedly and characteristically English and had added to itself some peculiarities unknown to continental Calvinism such as rigid Sabbatarianism; "the English Sunday" was already at war with the idea of Merrie England.

The Puritans did not object to physical exercise as such, and certainly not to physical training. John Milton in his essay "Of Education" recommended that three and a half hours each day should be devoted to boys' exercise, most of it in the form of military drill. Even sport might have its uses. "It were happy for the commonwealth if our magistrates would take into their care . . . the managing of our public sports and festival pastimes . . . such as may inure and harden our bodies by martial exercises to all warlike skill and performance." It was not sporting activity but the attitude to sport as an occasion for pleasure and joy in physical activity without regard to its utility which excited the disapproval of Puritans.

The contrast and the conflict between extreme views on sport of courtier and Puritan became acute at the beginning of the seventeenth century. James I carried on the Tudor royal patronage of sport and introduced Londoners to a sport of his own, pall-mall, and in his own little book *Basilicon Doron* dedicated "to Henrie my dearest son and natural successor" he appeared as a champion of sports—apart from football which was in his view "meeter for laming than for making abel the users thereof." Realizing, however, that Puritans were making attacks on sport and were coming near to persecuting those who practised them especially on Sundays James issued in 1618 his Declaration on Lawful Sports. Having already personally rebuked some "Puritans and precise people" in Lancashire for prohibiting and unlawfully punishing his good people for using their lawful recreations and honest exercises upon Sundays and other Holy Days after the afternoon sermon, he published a declaration pointing out the military value of sport, the danger of tippling and other vices if sport were denied to people and the impossibility of ordinary folk's enjoying sport at any other time except Sundays and Holy Days: "As for our good people's lawful recreation our pleasure likewise is, that after the end of divine service, our good people be not disturbed, letted or discouraged from any lawful recreation such as dancing, either men or women, archery for men, leaping, vaulting or any other such harmless recreation."

Certain sports including bull- and bear-baiting and bowling "for the meaner sort of people" were still prohibited. Recusants and those who did not go to church were denied the privilege of Sunday games. The same declaration was reissued by Charles I in 1633 and Archbishop Laud decreed that it should be read in all pulpits.

Sunday pastimes, however, had been forbidden by Parliamentary statute and the declaration was read under protest. One Puritan priest concluded by declaring: "You have heard read, good people, both the commandment of God and the commandment of man. Obey which you please." In the diocese of Norwich thirty parochial ministers were expelled for refusing to read the declaration, and the title page of an early edition states that the declaration led to Laud's execution. Thus sport was brought fully into the realm of politics as well as religion.

The lengths to which the Puritans went in their abhorrence of sport and its pleasures are shown in a confession of John Bunyan. Hockey, dancing, and tipcat on the village green were to him sins: after hearing a sermon against games and dancing he nevertheless yielded to temptation.

I shook the sermon out of my mind and to my old custom of sports and gaming I returned with great delight. But the same day as I was in the midst of a game of cat and having struck it one blow from the hole, just as I was about to strike it a second time, a voice did suddenly dart from heaven into my soul, which said "Wilt thou leave thy sins and go to heaven or have thy sins and go to Hell?" At this I was put in an exceeding maze; wherefore, leaving my cat upon the ground, I looked up to heaven and was as if I had with the eyes of my understanding seen the Lord Jesus looking down upon me, as being hotly displeased with me, and as if he did threaten me with some grievous punishment for those and other ungodly practices.

Such was Puritanism in its strength and its weakness. Notwithstanding the Anglican and liberal reaction and the Restoration of 1660 the ban on Sunday games substantially survived and the Puritans left their mark on English sport in permanence. Indeed, it was not until industrial and economic conditions made it possible to have a half-holiday on Saturday that sport for the masses came to be revived.

BIBLIOGRAPHY

1. BURCKHARDT, J., *The Civilization of the Renaissance in Italy* (London ed. 1945).
2. HEYWOOD, W., *Palio and Ponte*, p. 115 (London, 1904).
3. HUNT, R. W. *et al.*, *Studies in Medieval History*, pp. 358–60 (Oxford, 1948).
4. MARSHALL, JULIAN, *Annals of Tennis* (London, 1878).
5. HYMA, A., *The Youth of Erasmus*, p. 178 (Michigan, 1956).
See also
EINSTEIN, L., *The Italian Renaissance in England* (New York, 1902).
FUNCK-BRENTANO, F., *The Renaissance*, trans. F. C. Fletcher (London, 1936).
MILTON, J., *Of Education*
JAMES I, *Book of Lawful Sports*, 1618 and 1633 (reprinted Quaritch, London 1860).

V

PHILOSOPHERS AND SPORT

JOHN BUNYAN was thrown into prison in 1660 when the Restoration put an end to a period of military dictatorship and at the same time gave power to cavalier gentlemen and clergy to oppress dissenters. Suppression of the extreme Puritans did not have the effect of stamping out their attitude to life, nor did it do much to rehabilitate games and sports. More significant for sport in the long run were the activities of scientists and philosophers who sought to establish the autonomy of reason above the dogma of books and institutions. In the same year in which Bunyan was imprisoned Robert Boyle published his *New Experiments Physico-mechanical touching the Spring of Air and its Effects*. A Jesuit critic objected to this publication and while answering him Boyle enunciated Boyle's Law which perhaps symbolizes as well as any single event the progress of science at that date. When the Royal Society of London for Improving Natural Knowledge was founded, also in 1660, Kepler had already enunciated his laws relating to the motion of the planets and Harvey had discovered the circulation of the blood. Boyle himself made experiments in physiology but was hampered by "the tenderness of his nature" which "kept him from anatomical dissections." The Royal Society, before being incorporated under royal charter by Charles II, had been in existence for some years. Known as the "Invisible College," it had consisted of a band of inquiries interested in the "new philosophy" and met sometimes in Oxford but more frequently at Gresham's College in London.

The advance of science had no immediate impact upon the practice of sport nor directly upon social attitudes towards it. Nevertheless, the observation and objective analysis of physical phenomena including the functions of the human body contributed ultimately towards a new respect for physical function and performance. Perhaps more important was the renewed interest in metaphysics and the problem of knowledge, for metaphysics and physics were closely linked. Boyle learned Syriac, Greek and Hebrew in order to study the scriptures and had cogent statements to make about God as well as about gas. The philosopher Descartes, too, who advanced the ontological argument for the existence of God, was as much a physicist, a psychologist and a mathematician as he was a metaphysician.

At the beginning of the century metaphysics was still in the grip of a dualism which separated mind from matter and under the influence of Christian theologians had often exaggerated a distinction into an antagonism. Under such a metaphysic body and soul were seen as warring parties with the body as the villain of the piece. A re-examination of Platonic and Aristotelian sources did something to rehabilitate the body and bodily activity. The humanist educators had paid much attention to physical education. Michel de Montaigne in the sixteenth century stated with some force, "it is not a mind, it is not a body that we are training; it is a man and he ought not to be divided into two parts."[1] "The body," he said, "has a great share in our being, it has an eminent place there; and therefore its structure and composition very properly receive consideration."[2] These propositions were not perhaps very profound and certainly did not imply a fundamental rejection of dualism. They did, however, show that Montaigne was prepared to accord a new status to physical activity and was thinking of a Platonic rather than a monastic asceticism or training.

Moreover, Montaigne was concerned about the debilitating effect of the education of his day. In France, as elsewhere in Europe, the education of scholars was sharply distinguished from that of gentlemen. Scholars were educated in grammar schools, colleges and universities while gentlemen were taught in "academies" founded for the purpose. If gentlemen proceeded to the universities they would go to private teachers in the university cities in order to continue their training in social accomplishments. Both forms of education came under attack from Montaigne for their lack of attention to the body: "It is not enough to toughen his spirit, his muscles also must be toughened. For the spirit is too greatly strained if it is not supported and would have too hard a task to discharge two offices alone."[3]

Descartes, who was born four years after Montaigne died, preserved the dualism of mind and body. He tried to explain physiological phenomena mechanically and gave to the mind, as "a thinking substance," a status different from any other "extended substances" including human bodies. He fell back upon the miraculous intervention of God to synchronize body and soul. In England John Locke was profoundly influenced by both Montaigne and Descartes and especially by the former and did not depart from their fundamental philosophical dualism. He accepted, too, the need to teach young gentlemen the physical accomplishments of "good breeding." He was concerned about the effeteness of the aristocracy and advocated riding because it could be learned in towns and "is one of the best exercises for health which is to be had in those places of ease and luxury." Education should, in his view, be tough physically as well as mentally demanding. Locke's definition of recreation is interesting in that he rejected the concept of it as mere recovery from illness and returned to the Aristotelian concept of relaxation (ἀνάπαυσις): "Recreation," he said, "is not being idle (as everyone may observe) but easing the wearied part by change of business." "A gentleman's more serious employment I look on to be study; and when that demands relaxation and refreshment, it should be in some exercise of the body which unbends the body and confirms the health and strength."[4] He thus clearly accepted the dualism of mind and body and accorded physical recreation no higher place than that of a means to the end of "more serious employment."

The thinkers of the seventeenth century who provided a philosophical justification for sport in its own right were Spinoza and Leibniz. Spinoza attempted what none of the scientists or philosophers of the age had done, a synthesis of reality, a bridging of the gap between the natural and supernatural. In making this attempt he was inevitably led to reconsider the relationship between body and soul. Their apparent intimate relationship had puzzled philosophers and had led Descartes to produce his *Deus ex machina*. Materialists tried to explain away the soul and idealists the body. Spinoza, while recognizing a difference between mental and physical events, conceived of man as a finite mode of God both physical and mental, functioning in both ways at once—

> Body and mind are one of the same thing, conceived first under the attribute of thought, secondly under the attribute of extension. Thus it follows that the order or concatenation of things is identical, whether nature be conceived under one attribute or the other; consequently the order of states of activity and passivity in our body is simultaneous in nature with the order of states of activity and passivity in the mind.[5]

The philosophy of Spinoza provided no ground for denigrating or subordinating self-realization through physical activity. Although he himself perforce lived frugally he did not despise the joys and pleasures of life. On the contrary, he said, "it is the part of a wise man to use the world and delight himself in it as best he may, though not to satiety, for that is no delight."

When Spinoza tried to publish his views in Amsterdam in 1675 there was a storm of protest from Cartesian philosophers as well as from theologians and clergy, yet his long-term influence on metaphysics and on social and political philosophy was profound. Through Rousseau who read his works and developed some of his theories in the following century, his influence upon attitudes to sport, especially popular sport, was also considerable.

Leibniz, like Spinoza, rejected Descartes' separation of things into two heterogeneous substances only connected by the omnipotence of God, but he differed from Spinoza in his conception of what the true nature of substance was. Substance, for Leibniz, the ultimate reality, could only be conceived as force. For him there was no separation and certainly no antagonism between body and soul. Soul and body together made a living being and as their laws were in perfect harmony the results were the same as if one influenced the other. Thus the body did not act on the soul in the production of cognition, nor the soul on the body in the production of motion. The body acted just as if it had no soul and the soul as as if it had no body.[6] Here, too, was a metaphysic not hostile to physical activity and sport although Leibniz himself was not interested in this sphere of activity.

In England the writings of Berkeley and Hume also prepared the way for new developments in social attitudes to sport. Both these philosophers concentrated their energies upon the problem of "knowing." David Hume seemed to exhaust and perhaps explode the possibilities of valid knowledge of the outside world. "The idea of substance," he wrote, "is nothing but a collection of simple ideas that are united by imagination and have a particular name assigned to them." The concept of cause and effect was in Hume's view not a product of reason at all. No belief could be proved but "belief is more properly an act of the sensitive than the cognitive part of our natures." Again "we believe not because we can prove our opinions but because we cannot help believing."[7] Whether or not Hume's view can be justified has been questioned and disputed. There is less doubt on the historical thesis that he effectively prepared the way for the reinstatement of sensation and the emotions and so made the Romantics in philosophy, in literature and in art more acceptable to educated and thinking men.

Before considering the particular contribution of Rousseau to the philosophy of sport it is necessary to cast a glance at the ways in which men were in fact disporting themselves during the Age of Enlightenment. The Restoration of 1660 in its social aspect restored the nobles and the gentry once more as the acknowledged leaders of local and national life.

Charles II re-established the court and, to some extent, courtly modes of behaviour but the influence of the gentry, and the country squirearchy was strong and when the non-English-speaking Hanoverians ascended the throne at the beginning of the eighteenth century, the country house and town house took precedence over the palace as the arbiters of taste and fashion. A symptom of the growing power of the squirearchy in Parliament and in the country at large was the enactment of the Game Laws during the Restoration period. The Forest Laws of Norman and Plantaganet times had assured the king of plenty of deer to hunt. Now in 1671 Parliament passed a law which prevented all freeholders of under a hundred pounds a year from killing "game" even on their own land. This meant considerable hardship for many countrymen and yeomen farmers. The very use of the term *game* flaunted the sports of the gentry in the faces of country-men who needed the food rather than the sport afforded by the game on their land. Fox-hunting began to take on a modern appearance in this period. The Civil War had been responsible for the opening up of deer parks, and decimating the herds. Now foxes, instead of being killed indiscriminately as vermin, began to be hunted with packs of hounds by the gentry across the country at large, irrespective of its ownership. Hunting the hare was apparently the one form of hunting which was "popular" in the sense that all classes shared in the pursuit and the fun.

The patronage of Newmarket by Charles II gave horse-racing a filip. He himself became known as Old Rowley after his favourite hack and won the Town Plate on more than one occasion. The interest of the Stuarts was continued by Queen Anne, who took a pride in the improvement of her horse-racing stud. In her time the famous progenitors of English bloodstock, the Darley Arabian, the Godolphin Arabian and the Byerly Turk were introduced. Another activity which was increasingly patronized by the gentry, if not by royalty, was cricket, and the eighteenth century was the golden age of the Hambledon Club on Broad Halfpenny Down.

Meanwhile the commons amused themselves in a variety of pastimes, in wrestling under different rules in different parts of the country, in primitive forms of football or "hurling", in "pedestrian" feats and races, in animal-baiting, and, of course, in dancing especially at the hundreds of fairs which were held up and down the country. Popular sport, when it did not hang around the fringes of the gentry's pastimes, was primitive and not well organized.

In the towns in the eighteenth century conditions were so rough that a premium was placed on an ability to protect life, limbs and property. The classical age of Samuel Johnson, of Gibbon and of Burke was one in which Hogarth, Fielding and Smollett found many abuses to expose. In the early decades of the century the death-rate rose rapidly and passed the birth-rate. Gin drinking was encouraged and doubtless the demand for corn for distilling was good for the landed interest. At the height of the gin era in 1740–2 burials in London were twice as numerous as baptisms, and Hogarth vividly depicted the horrors of Gin Street in contrast with the prosperity of Beer Street. Violence was, not unnaturally, a feature of the age which boasted two hundred capital offences at law and was taken for granted in daily life. In 1780 the Gordon rioters burned seventy houses and four gaols in London.

So it was that James Figg who kept the "Adam and Eve" in what is now Tottenham Court Road, taught to young bucks "Ye Noble Science of Defence"—no sport this, but a realistic form of fighting with cudgel and fist. The activity first adopted the guise of sport when Figg claimed to be a "champion" and was challenged by one, Sutton, of Gravesend. The fighters drank a bottle of port in the single fifteen-minute interval and Figg won.

Figg was succeeded by Jack Broughton whose great contribution was to draw up the Broughton Rules in 1741, which were generally accepted for sporting contests for nearly a century. He also introduced gloves for sparring but not for contests. Boxing was, nevertheless, a sport begotten by the social conditions of the age, vigorous and tough but often brutal and lacking the dignity and skill of other combat sports in other times. It was patronized by the gentry as spectators— in 1750 the Duke of Cumberland wagered Lord Chesterfield £10,000 to £400 on Jack Broughton and lost!—but they did not often enter the ring as participants. The distinction between noble and ignoble sports was as clearly marked in the eighteenth century as at any time.

The writer who did more than any other to change social attitudes to sport was J. J. Rousseau. His political philosophy had a tremendous impact upon the practice of democracy, and of government, but it was in his educational tract *Émile*, published in 1762, that he indicated clearly the implications of his naturalistic philosophy for sport. He saw more than Locke did in games of skill. Training for stamina, and the acquisition of social accomplishments had their place but through physical skills Émile above all would learn about the mechanics of the world and about himself. He would satisfy, too, his natural desire for physical movement and achievement. Education according to nature was a development of Spinoza's theory of self-realization. The child must be given activities which would satisfy his desires and aspirations at his particular stage of development. Games and sports also had their therapeutic value and Émile was to have provided for him activities in which he would lose "all the dangerous inclinations that spring from idleness."

The idea of character-training through physical activity which was to find such strong support in the nineteenth century was signposted by Rousseau—

> The training of the body, though much neglected is . . . the most important part of education not only for making children healthy and robust, but even more for the moral effect, which is generally neglected altogether or sought by teaching the child a number of pedantic precepts that are only so many mis-spent words.

An even more significant theory and one which has often been overlooked was Rousseau's proposition that sport could and should be used for political and nationalistic ends. Such was Rousseau's reputation as an authority on social and political philosophy that he was invited to give advice upon the reconstituted state of Poland. Accordingly in 1773 he published *Considerations on the Government of Poland.*[8] Having stated that men's souls should be given a national patriotic stamp through the impact of education he went on to suggest that sport had a special role to play in the production of patriots. Games were to make children's "hearts glow and create a deep love for the fatherland and its laws"—

> The children should not be permitted to play separately according to their fancy, but encouraged to play all together in public; and the games should be conducted in such a way that there is always some common end to which all aspire to accustom them to common action and to stir up emulation. The parents who would rather have domestic education, and want their children

brought up under their own supervision ought, nevertheless, to send them to these exercises. Their instruction may be got at home and adapted to individual need, but their games should always be played in public and shared by all. It is not merely a question of keeping them busy, or of cultivating a sound constitution and making them alert and graceful. The important thing is to get them accustomed from an early age to discipline, to equality and fraternity, to living under the eyes of their fellow citizens and seeking public approbation.

This advice was given to Poland in the eighteenth century, but in the following century it was taken and acted upon in Sweden, Denmark, Germany and the United States.

Even before the end of the century Rousseau's educational theories were being tried in Germany by J. B. Basedow in his *Philanthropinum* in Dessau. New schools were founded on the pattern of this prototype and, at one of them at Schnepfenthal, Guts Muths gave excellent service in physical education for nearly fifty years. From here ideas on education, including views on the use of sport for popular physical education, spread to Denmark, where they influenced Franz Nachtegall, and to Sweden, where they inspired P. H. Ling. In Germany, too, F. L. Jahn developed from them his crusade for *Turnen*, while in Switzerland they greatly influenced Pestalozzi who became the most famous school-teacher in Europe. In Denmark, Sweden and Germany a preoccupation with nationalism and with physical and moral regeneration after the disastrous defeats of the Napoleonic wars transmuted a movement in favour of sport into a rigid system of gymnastics. Both Guts Muths and P. H. Ling were as interested in sport as in gymnastics and Guts Muths wrote a book on *Games* analysing one hundred and five of them according to the skills which they developed. Ling, too, was interested in sport, especially in fencing, riding and swimming. It was, however, the systems of gymnastics of these two pioneers which met the political needs of their time and it was as gymnastic theorists that they were subsequently remembered.

In Great Britain, where for two years from 1765 David Hume had offered a home of refuge to Rousseau, the influence of the French philosopher was more subtle and perhaps more far-reaching. His educational theories were not deliberately applied, except in a few schools, and popular education made a slow start in the nineteenth century. When it did it was not noticeably on naturalistic lines. On the other hand the growth of organized games and the cult of athleticism at Public Schools quickly made character-training its *raison d'être* and showed how, for one section of society at least, sport could be used to accustom boys "to common action and to stir up emulation" and to promote national solidarity and patriotism. Across the Atlantic, also, it was sport rather than gymnastics which made the more significant contribution to the American way of life.

BIBLIOGRAPHY

1. DE MONTAIGNE, MICHEL, *Essays*, I, 145, ed. W. C. Hazlitt (London, 1923).
2. DE MONTAIGNE, MICHEL, *Essays*, II, 303, ed. W. C. Hazlitt (London, 1923).
3. DE MONTAIGNE, MICHEL, *Essays*, I, 133, ed. W. C. Hazlitt (London, 1923).
4. LOCKE, JOHN, *Some Thoughts Concerning Education*, p. 153 (London, 1883).
5. DE SPINOZA, B., *The Ethics*, Part III, Proposition 2, note, trans. Hale White and A. H. Stirling (London, 1899).
6. LEIBNIZ, G. W. VON, *Opera Philosophica*, ed. Erdmann, p. 711 (Berlin, 1840) *see* "Leibniz", *Encyclopaedia Britannica*.
7. HUME, D., *An Inquiry Concerning Human Understanding*, I, 4 (London, 1896).
8. ROUSSEAU, J. J., Considerations for the Government of Poland, in William Boyd, *The Minor Educational Writings of J. J. Rousseau* (London, 1911).

VI

ATHLETICISM: I

AT the beginning of the nineteenth century an attempt was made to import the German sport of *Turnen* into Britain. While Guts Muths had been almost exclusively concerned with the sport and physical education of children, J. F. C. L. Jahn envisaged a national sporting movement which would regenerate the German people after their disasters in the Napoleonic Wars and would establish their superiority over all other peoples. Undoubtedly the Germans had felt during the previous century an acute sense of military, political and cultural inferiority to France, and the Romantic Movement at the end of the century had excited many Germans with a new sense of purpose. When, in 1810, Jahn published his *Deutsches Volkstum*—The German Way of Life—it was an immediate success. Jahn himself became prominent and influential in public life. His gymnastics, first publicly demonstrated at the open-air gymnasium, *Turnplatz*, in the Hasenheide in 1811, spread rapidly throughout Germany and had strong military and political connexions. He himself wrote—

> Only when all men of military age have become capable, through physical education of bearing arms, have become ready for combat through weapon training, prompt to strike through new kinds of war games and constant alertness, and battle keen through love of the Fatherland—only then can a people be called militarily prepared.[1]

The popularity of Jahn's movement and his abuse of the establishment brought him into conflict with von Kamptz, chief of police to the Prussian state. In 1819 the movement was suppressed and a number of gymnasia were closed down. It was then that one of Jahn's pupils, Carl Voelker, came to London to try out *Turnen* in a slightly more liberal environment. He sought and obtained the support of the founder of the utilitarian school of philosophy, Jeremy Bentham, and of Lord Brougham. A *Turnplatz* was opened at No. 1 Union Place, New Road, near Regent's Park. Exercises on horizontal and parallel bars, rope- and ladder-climbing and pole-vaulting across trenches made a strong appeal initially and a second *Turnplatz* was opened in Finsbury Square. Here, John Neal, an American man of letters, took lessons and became so enthusiastic about *Turnen* that he recommended the employment in America of another of Jahn's disciples, Francis Lieber. Yet neither in Britain nor in America did *Turnen* really thrive although they had a considerably greater impact across the Atlantic than in Britain. The fact was that this foreign graft was incompatible with the root stock of British sport in its particular state of growth at the beginning of the century and, too, with the multifarious new scions of sport which sprouted during it.

In 1800 the British aristocracy enjoyed the country life as much as, if not more than, they enjoyed town life. An essential part of this life was sport. The great number of sporting prints and pictures dating from the early nineteenth century bear witness to a love of outdoor life and pursuits. Indeed, there was a tendency for the word *sport* to be identified with field sports while the word *game* was used to denote the birds and animals which provided the sport. The aristocracy were only partially successful in appropriating these words for their exclusive use, nevertheless the word *sport* still has in the twentieth century this association with the old field sports.

Hunting, shooting and angling were the aristocratic rural sports. Hunting on horseback was particularly suited to the newly enclosed and drained countryside. The rural population was rigidly excluded from these sports by the Game Laws. It was illegal to buy or sell game. It was illegal for anyone not a squire or a squire's eldest son to kill game even at the invitation of the landowner. This prohibition was abolished by law in 1831 in spite of the opposition of the Duke of Wellington. However, another law had been passed in 1816 making any cottager who was caught netting hares or rabbits liable to transportation for seven years. Such laws were not enforced without difficulty. Pitched battles with shotguns between poachers and landlords' forces sometimes developed and it was not until 1827 that mantraps and spring-guns which might kill or maim an unwary trespasser were made illegal.

In another category of sport came golf and cricket. Both games had been adopted from the countryside by the aristocracy and were organized under their patronage. The Marylebone Cricket Club and the Royal and Ancient Golf Club at St. Andrews were not set up to govern or organize their respective sports, but, because of the prestige of their members, they were called in to settle disputes or to draw up agreements on rules or etiquette and gradually assumed control. Neither cricket nor golf was exclusively aristocratic, but at the beginning of the century they did not boast a great many players or spectators.

The sports which drew the crowds were horse-racing, prize-fighting and pedestrian feats of walking or running. Horse-racing had risen to fame at Newmarket under the patronage of Charles II. Throughout the eighteenth century racing grew in popularity and other courses and meetings were founded on the model of Newmarket. By the end of the century three of the five great classic races had been founded, the St. Leger at Doncaster in 1778 and the Oaks and the Derby at Epsom in 1779 and 1780. The Two Thousand Guineas was first run at Newmarket in 1809 and the One Thousand Guineas in 1814. The list was then complete.

Great crowds of ten and twenty thousand would assemble to watch, to trade and to gamble, yet the sport of horse-racing was well controlled by the Jockey Club. The club had started about 1750 as an informal dining club of gentlemen who had an interest in racing at Newmarket. Gradually it became the arbiter in all disputes. Its prestige and power grew so that in 1791 when Sam Chiffney, the jockey of the Prince Regent, was suspected of rigging two races, the prince himself, who was not above suspicion of complicity was warned off the course by the Jockey Club which used the simple expedient of telling him that no gentleman would start against him so long as he employed Sam Chiffney.

Prize-fights also drew large crowds and there was a complete mixture of classes. Lord Althorp speaking of his youth said that " his conviction of the advantages of boxing had been so strong that he had been seriously considering whether it was not a duty he owed to the public to go and attend every prize-fight which took place . . . He described a fight between Gully and the Chicken. How he rode down to Brickhill—how he was loitering about the inn door when a barouche-and-four drove up with Lord Byron and a party and Jackson the trainer—how they all dined together, and how pleasant it had been. Then the fight the next day; the men stripping, the intense excitement, the sparring; then the first round, the attitude of the men—it was really worthy of Homer."[2] George IV at his coronation in 1820 had had a guard of honour of prize-fighters led by Gentleman John Jackson.

Pedestrian feats, runs or long-distance walks, sometimes against an opponent, and sometimes against the clock but always for a wager were daily announced in the sporting Press. Some of these pedestrians were tradesmen or poor people, others were members of the nobility. One of the most notable was Captain Barclay Allardice who was a Scottish landowner drawing as much as £3,000 a year from his estates. By 1808 he had a number of athletic feats to his credit and in that year he accepted a wager to go on foot one thousand miles in one thousand successive hours at the rate of one mile in each and every hour for a wager of one thousand guineas. He began his walk on 1st June, 1809, on Newmarket Heath without previous specific training. He completed this extraordinary performance on 12th July more than two stone lighter in weight but still in good fettle so that five days later he was able to join the military expedition to Walcheren as aide-de-camp to the Marquis of Huntly. Towards the end of his walk crowds of spectators came from all directions and there was not a bed to be had in Newmarket, or Cambridge or in any of the neighbouring towns and villages.

The lower ranks of society had a number of indigenous and local sports. At fairs up and down the country, after the trading had been done and the labourers had been hired for the season, there would be athletic competitions of various kinds for young men and women. The events were of a spontaneous nature. In some parts of the country mob football was popular, a violent and damaging game, unregulated by any code of laws and often using the main street of the village as its terrain after shopkeepers had put up their shutters. Industrial urbanization was beginning, but not even London was so large that the inhabitants could not escape on their holidays to some sporting event on the outskirts.

Such was the pattern of sport in England at the beginning of the century. By the end the pattern was vastly different. Field sports still had their narrow aristocratic following, although the aristocracy had been augmented by many new members. Horse-racing flourished and drew the crowds that it always had done. Cricket and golf were being played by many more people from all ranks of society and both games supported a fairly large body of professional players and teachers. Pedestrianism and the prize-ring had gone altogether. Prize-fighting had always been susceptible to abuse, and in the nineteenth century the increase of corruption, the buying of fights, and the vicious nature of the fights themselves brought the whole sport into disrepute so that it was suppressed. A new start had to be made for boxing by the Marquess of Queensberry who formulated new rules in 1866. Pedestrianism, too, suffered from similar abuses so that gentlemen ceased to find the events congenial to them whether as competitors or spectators. Later in the century the gentlemen founded their own athletic association in order to start athletics afresh without any of the abuses which were rife in pedestrianism. It is probably not without significance that the sports which survived were those enjoying the patronage of the aristocracy who had turned themselves and their social gatherings at Newmarket, at Marylebone and at St. Andrews into organizations which were ready to lay down the law and enforce it. The Pugilistic Club formed in 1814 never assumed the functions or the social status of the M.C.C., the Jockey Club or the R. and A. Where the aristocracy did not organize themselves into a controlling club as in pedestrianism or pugilism they failed as individuals to keep the rough and unscrupulous elements in check and the sports died.

Two of the most remarkable features in nineteenth-century sport were the great proliferation of sports and their organization under effective governing bodies. Table I illustrates both these trends.

To understand the nature of the changes that took place a start can be made with Matthew Arnold's "humble attempt at a scientific nomenclature" for the structure of society—Barbarians, Philistines and Populace. The nomenclature was hardly complimentary but then Matthew Arnold devoted his life to infusing "sweetness and light" into a society which from top to bottom seemed to him to be lacking both those ingredients of culture. Barbarians were the upper class who did, indeed, have a kind of image or shadow of sweetness but were seduced away from the light by the charms of worldly splendour, security, power and pleasure. Nevertheless, they had cultivated a staunch individualism and had

TABLE I
The Organization of Sport

Sport	Earliest National Organisation	Date
Horse-racing	Jockey Club	c. 1750
Golf	Royal and Ancient Golf Club	1754
Cricket	Marylebone Cricket Club	1788
Mountaineering	Alpine Club	1857
Association Football	Football Association	1863
Athletics	Amateur Athletic Club	1866
	Amateur Athletic Association	1880
Swimming	Amateur Metropolitan Swimming Association	1869
Rugby Football	Rugby Football Union	1871
Sailing	Yacht Racing Association	1875
Cycling	Bicyclists' Union	1878
Skating	National Skating Association	1879
Rowing	Metropolitan Rowing Association	1879
Boxing	Amateur Boxing Association	1884
Hockey	Hockey Association	1886
Lawn Tennis	Lawn Tennis Association	1888
Badminton	Badminton Association	1895
Fencing	Amateur Fencing Association	1898

asserted personal liberty of which there was, despite the Game Laws already mentioned, a very rich supply in English life. Philistines were the middle class to which Arnold himself claimed to belong—Philistine because the term gave the notion of something particularly stiffnecked and perverse in the resistance to light and its children. They preferred the "machinery of business, chapels, tea meetings and addresses from Mr. Murphy and the Rev. W. Cattle which makes up their dismal and illiberal life." Thirdly, there was the working class, raw and half developed, which by mid century was beginning to perplex Arnold and others by "marching where it likes, meeting where it likes, bawling what it likes, breaking what it likes."

One of the characteristics of the Barbarians recognized by Arnold was their passion for field sports. They were "of this passion too, as of the passion for asserting one's personal liberty, the great natural stronghold." Indeed, at the beginning of the century all that was prominent and all that was organized in British sport was Barbarian, but the Barbarians made no attempt to hand down their sports to the populace, nor to organize them for participation by a wider clientele. At the end of the century the pattern of sport was predominantly Philistine. The middle classes had produced their own team games such as football and hockey, their own form of track and field athletics, their own swimming competitions and their own racket game of lawn tennis. Rowing and cycling they organized, and into cricket they infiltrated in such numbers that they made it almost a middle-class game. Of all these activities only lawn tennis was invented by the middle class for the middle class. The other sports were discovered in an embryonic state and were developed and organized by the Philistines. The successful sports were all those that could be practised in or around the growing towns and cities, in suburban gardens, on quite small grass fields, in public parks, on rivers, in public swimming baths and on the public highway. Moreover, the Philistines after some initial reluctance to embrace the Populace in their sports did at last welcome them provided that the Populace would conform to their etiquette and conduct in play. Many Philistines went further and introduced games and sports to the Populace with a missionary zeal.

The first signs of the revolutionary change in sport appeared in the Public Schools and the Universities of Oxford and Cambridge. At the beginning of the century there were but seven boarding schools, Winchester, Westminster, Eton. Harrow, Charterhouse, Rugby and Shrewsbury, which answered to Sidney Smith's definition of a Public School as "an endowed place of education of old standing to which the sons of gentlemen resort in large numbers and where they continue to reside from eight or nine to eighteen years of age."[3] Between these Public Schools for the rich and the parochial schools for the poor were a number of commercial schools of doubtful efficiency and morality. The educational provision for the Philistines was quite inadequate, yet this class was growing in number and in power. In 1832, the year of the first Reform Bill, Dr. Thomas Arnold, the great headmaster of Rugby from 1828 to 1842 wrote two letters to *The Sheffield Courant* on "The Education of the Middle Classes" pointing out the woeful deficiency of schools. He did not specifically recommend that Rugby School should be copied elsewhere, but this is what happened. New schools were founded and old grammar schools were developed and expanded until by about 1860 the middle classes had by invasion and imitation forced their way into the educational preserves of the aristocracy.

The winning of educational privilege by the Philistines coincided with, and was responsible for, the growth of organized games, particularly cricket and football. Previously the schoolboy versions of Barbarian sports, hunting and shooting, had led to a notorious lawlessness in schools and in the countryside. Headmasters were hostile to sport. Dr. Keate at Eton tried to prevent cricket against Harrow; the head-master of Westminster tried to prevent rowing races with Eton and Dr. Butler, headmaster of Shrewsbury thought that football was "only fit for butcher boys." But boys organized their own sport in defiance of authority. The growth of the games cult is often attributed to Dr. Arnold of Rugby, but it was already advanced among boys at Rugby and elsewhere when Arnold became headmaster in 1828. Arnold himself was mildly interested in cricket and slightly more so in swimming, gymnastics and throwing the spear. He did not show any interest in the game of football, to which the school gave its name. He was not interested in athleticism and it is the fault of Thomas Hughes' novel *Tom Brown's Schooldays* that Arnold has so often been credited or debited with the cult of organized games.

What Arnold did do was to suppress lawlessness ruthlessly and thereby he also suppressed the Barbarian country pursuits and sports, disbanding the boys' pack of hounds and forbidding "hare and hounds." Boys turned more and more to those sports which were allowed. Furthermore, Arnold was determined to run the school through his praepostors. There was no sphere in which self-government by boys was so apt or so well developed as in games. So it was that the Headmaster of Harrow in evidence to the Royal Commission on the Public Schools 1860–4 could say: "I ought perhaps to conclude what has been said on this subject by explaining that fagging and compulsory attendance at football are parts of the internal government which was, so far as we know, originally established by the boys themselves, and is now certainly administered by them alone."

Lord Byron played cricket for Harrow against Eton in 1805. The Oxford and Cambridge cricket matches began in 1827 and the first university boat race was held two years later. What Arnold did was indirectly to accelerate a movement which had already begun and because of the fame of his school he unwittingly contributed no small part to the spread of football, especially of course, Rugby football. It was left to other headmasters to adopt and to encourage athleticism as an instrument of education. G. E. L. Cotton, who was one of Arnold's assistant masters, did so when headmaster of Marlborough and Edward Thring did likewise at Uppingham, taking part in the boys' games himself. But the trend was general after Arnold's death and by 1864 the Clarendon Commissioners could record that the cricket and football fields were not merely places of exercise and amusement; they helped to form some of the most valuable social qualities and manly virtues and they held, like the classroom and the boarding-house, a distinct and important place in Public School education.

By the 1860s the Philistine features were well established in sport at schools and universities. The Headmaster of Winchester who referred to "the idle boys, I mean the boys who play cricket" was succeeded by one who said: "Give me a boy who is a cricketer. I can make something of him." Football had been taken by the schools from the Populace and transformed by means of a number of different sets of rules from a test of brute strength into a game of skill. The foundation of the Football Association in 1863 marked the first step towards two great categories of kicking and carrying games. From the Barbarians the Philistines took hunting and steeplechasing, dispensed with the hounds and the horses and transformed the sports into harmless cross-country runs and hurdle-races for middle-class athletes. Etonians had their cross-country steeplechase on foot by 1845. In 1850 the undergraduates of Exeter College, Oxford, decided to adapt the college "grind" or steeplechase for human runners. They set up ten flights of agricultural hurdles three feet-six inches high, ten yards apart, which the athletes had to clear in a race of a hundred and forty yards. This was the first modern hurdle race.

The Philistines were not opposed to imports from abroad. At several schools and at Oxford a form of *Turnen* was practised by a few. Gymnastics, however, had to compete as a sport with other sports produced by the fertile imagination of the Philistines. It was an unequal struggle. Matthew Arnold, the son of the great Dr. Thomas Arnold, himself an inspector of schools and familiar with education in Germany, summed up the situation to the Taunton Commission in 1868. "Nothing however will make an ex-schoolboy of one of the great English schools regard the gymnastics of a foreign school without a slight feeling of wonder and compassion, so much more animating and interesting do the games of his remembrance seem to him."[4]

BIBLIOGRAPHY

1. JAHN, J. F. C. L., *Das Deutsche Volkstum* and DIXON J. G., Prussia, Politics and Physical Education, in *Landmarks in the History of Physical Education*, ed. P. C. McIntosh (London, 1957).
2. TREVELYAN, G. M., *English Social History* (London, 1944).
3. *Edinburgh Review*, Vol. 16, p. 326 (August, 1810).
4. TAUNTON COMMISSION, *Report of the Schools Inquiry Commission* (London, 1868).
  See also
    HUGHES, T., *Tom Brown's Schooldays* 1st ed. (London, 1857).
    MACK, E. C., *Public Schools and British Opinion, 1780–1860* (London, 1938).
    WORSLEY, T. C., *Barbarians and Philistines* (London, 1940).
    WYMER, N., *Dr. Arnold of Rugby* (London, 1953).
    YOUNG, G. M., *Early Victorian England* (1934).

VII

ATHLETICISM: II

DURING the second half of the nineteenth century the cult—for so it was—of team games and athletic sports spread far beyond the walls of schools and universities. It was in tune with much liberal thinking in politics, in literature and even in theology. Dr. Thomas Arnold had been a liberal schoolmaster, historian and churchman, and, although he did not consciously find a place for sport in his liberalism, other liberals, even liberal churchmen, did so.

John Henry Newman, who was forty-one years old when Arnold died, did not begin his career as a liberal. At Oxford he seemed to be afraid lest rationalistic liberalism might lose sight of profound Christian truths which had been derived from revelation and were preserved by the Church in her traditions. In later years his fears were quite different. Theological narrowness might rival liberalism as an opponent to Christianity.

In his lectures on *The Idea of a University* published in 1851 Cardinal Newman gave his own interpretation of liberalism. The fourth discourse entitled "Liberal Knowledge Its Own End" has much to say that justifies sport as a worthy, as well as a legitimate pursuit for mankind. Looking back to the ancient world Newman condemned Cato who "estimated everything by what it produced." He went on—

> Things which can bear to be cut off from everything else and yet persist in living must have life in themselves; pursuits which issue in nothing, and still maintain their grounds for ages, which are regarded as admirable, though they have not yet proved themselves to be useful, must have their sufficient end in themselves, whatever it turns out to be.

It was into this category of things which needed no justification outside themselves that Newman placed sport both ancient and modern. He was still a dualist in that he saw bodily and mental activity as sharply divided, but he was not prepared to confine the quality of liberality to intellectual activity—

> There is then a great variety of intellectual exercise which are not technically called liberal; on the other hand I say there are exercises of the body which do receive that appellation. Such, for instance, was the palaistra in ancient times; such the Olympic Games in which strength and dexterity of body as well as of mind gained the prize.

Looking at the sport of his own day he did not accord to it the honour and glory of a Pindar, but in a revealing passage he rejected the need to justify sport by its utility. There might indeed be a scale of values for ends and the end of sport might be lower in the scale than some intellectual or contemplative activities, but at least sport was an end in itself deserving the appellation liberal—

> Manly games, or games of skill, or military prowess, though bodily, are, it seems, accounted liberal; on the other hand what is merely professional, though highly intellectual, nay, though liberal in comparison of trade and manual labour, is not simply called liberal, and mercantile occupations are not liberal at all. Why this distinction? Because that alone is liberal knowledge which stands on its own pretensions, which is independent of sequel, expects no complement, refuses to be *informed* (as it is called) by any end, or absorbed into any art, in order duly to present itself to our contemplation. The most ordinary pursuits have this specific character if they are self-sufficient and complete; the highest lose it if they minister to something beyond them. It is absurd to balance, in point of worth and importance, a treatise on reducing fractures with a game of cricket or a fox chase; yet of the two, the bodily exercise has that quality which we call liberal and the intellectual has it not.

Nevertheless, sport depended for its liberality upon the

way in which it was done. Social attitudes change from time
to time. The *palaestra* was liberal to Lycurgus in the eighth
century B.C. but not to Seneca in the first century A.D.
Chariot-racing and combat sports were liberal at Olympia in
500 B.C. but not in the England of 1851. Whenever personal
gain was the motive the character of the pursuit was altered
and it ceased to be liberal. "Thus racing," he wrote, "which
was a liberal exercise in Greece, forfeits its rank in times like
these, so far as it is made the occasion of gambling." How well
this fitted the conception of the gentleman amateur which the
Philistines were even then formulating. Gambling had never
been thought by the Barbarians to be an improper adjunct to
sport but the governing bodies of amateur sports which were
set up from 1863 onwards invariably prohibited the laying of
bets and wagers.

There was a number of churchmen whose devotion to
sport and whose advocacy of it in novels and essays earned
them the name "muscular Christians." Charles Kingsley and
Thomas Hughes were among them. *Westward Ho* was
published in 1855 and *Tom Brown's Schooldays* in 1857. In
both books the heroes were drawn in glowing colours and
were intended to display the excellence of simple understanding and unconscious instinct to do good. They were, moreover, adorned with every sort of athletic accomplishment.
For Tom Brown and one of his schoolmasters with whom he
conversed, cricket was a noble game, but more than a game,
an institution, the birthright of British boys old and young,
as habeas corpus and trial by jury are of British men. The
exercise of unselfishness was particularly ennobling and that
was why the team games of cricket and football were "such
much better games than fives, or hare and hounds or any
others where the object is to come in first and to win for
oneself and not that one's side may win." Tom did not add
what later observers thought, namely that the team games

encouraged just those qualities of co-operation and conformity to the needs of the herd which were so much prized by a middle class which was establishing its power and influence throughout the world.

In a later book, *The Manliness of Christ*, Hughes regretted the lengths to which athleticism had gone. There is no doubt that he himself was partly responsible and that the churches provided the focal points for a vast number of sports clubs during the 1870s. In 1874 young men connected with Aston Villa Wesleyan Chapel in a suburb of Birmingham formed a club to play football on Saturday afternoons. Aston Villa Football Club soon outgrew and abandoned the chapel which had fostered it. In the same year Bolton Wanderers started as Christ Church Football Club. Wolverhampton Wanderers (1877), Everton (1878), Queen's Park Rangers (1885), South-ampton (1885) and Barnsley (1887) are a few of the now more famous clubs which were started or encouraged by some young curate or minister anxious to introduce football to the young men in his congregation, but hundreds of humbler clubs were started in the same way. A survey of football clubs which had come into existence by 1880 in Birmingham and district shows that of three hundred and forty-four clubs eighty-three, or twenty-four per cent are known to have been connected with church, chapel or religious organization. Many more whose origin is obscure were almost certainly similarly connected. The comparable figure for cricket clubs is twenty-one per cent.[1] Puritanism prevented these games being played on Sunday and undoubtedly coloured the views of many who welcomed sport as the least of the evils that beset the urban populace or as an attraction which might well divert them from vice. Others both inside and outside the churches were only too glad to embrace sport as an innocent source of pleasure and satisfaction for the masses.

The promotion of sport by churches and churchmen was

dependent upon the economic growth of the community and an increase in leisure. These factors, too, turned Newman's liberal view of sport from an academic theory with few practical applications beyond the lower fringe of the upper middle class into a philosophy of action for the Populace. The extension of middle-class sport to the working classes took place for the most part during the two decades from 1870 to 1890 and coincided with a successful campaign fought by clerks and artisans for a reduction in working hours.

As early as 1848 the building trades had secured a "four o'clock Saturday" in some towns but most workers had to wait until the 1870s before they enjoyed a weekly half-holiday. Speaking of the early 1860s George Cadbury, founder of the Birmingham cocoa and chocolate firm said—

> Our working times at that time were from eight o'clock in the morning until seven thirty in the evening, Saturdays included. There was no factory in Birmingham, so far as I know, that closed on Saturday afternoons and I believe we were the first to close at midday on Saturdays: people told us it would mean ruin.[2]

It certainly did not mean ruin for the firm of Cadbury. By about 1870 in many parts of the country a campaign by workers for a shorter working day—the nine hours' day at this time—became irresistible. This meant that for many workers in industry and business the working week was reduced by six hours. The clerks were the first to have increased leisure concentrated on Saturday afternoon but manual workers soon achieved the same concession. It was then, and only then, that the great proliferation of sports clubs and district organizations took place.

The popularity of association football almost certainly exceeded that of any other sport both in terms of participants and spectators. The Football Association was founded in 1863. There were then ten member clubs. The number had risen to fifty in 1871 and ten thousand one hundred in 1905. The first

F

challenge cup competition was played in 1871–2. The attendances at the final then and in later years speak for themselves—

1871–2 at Kennington Oval	2,000
1880–1 at Kennington Oval	4,000
1890–1 at Kennington Oval	23,000
1900–1 at Crystal Palace	110,802

But association football and cricket were not alone. The survey
of Birmingham and district shows that Rugby football, roller
skating, track and field athletics and cross-country running
developed early in the seventies, while cycling, swimming
lawn tennis and boxing came into fashion later. Birmingham
may be considered typical of the new industrial towns. By
1890 the Philistine's revolution of sport had determined the
pattern of organization, the laws and the techniques both for
themselves and for the Populace.

Matthew Arnold had published his own views on the
revolution in its early years. *Culture and Anarchy* appeared in
1869. He was the eldest son of Thomas Arnold and had a
profound respect for his father. He also drew heavily upon
Newman, and like him set himself against the utilitarian view
of education as the training of men to carry out particular
tasks for society. He did not, however, agree with Newman
about the justification of sport as an end in itself. "Population," he wrote in *Culture and Anarchy*, "and bodily health
and vigour are things which are nowhere treated in such an
unintelligent, misleading, exaggerated way as in England.
Both are really machinery; yet how many people all around
us do we see rest in them and fail to look beyond them."[3]

He admitted that bodily health and vigour had a more real
and essential value than, for instance, wealth, which was
machinery and never anything but machinery, but they only
had value when intimately connected with a spiritual condition. Here he became slightly equivocal about the justification

of bodily exercise as an end in itself. At this point in the argument he did in fact talk about bodily exercise and not about sport although it seemed to be sport which he had in mind. One thing about which he was clear was that the Philistines of his day fell within Epictetus' definition of *unculture* because they gave themselves up to things which related to the body, made a great fuss about exercise, a great fuss about eating, a great fuss about drinking, a great fuss about walking, a great fuss about riding, whereas the formation of the spirit and character should have been their real concern.

Muscular Christians, far from realizing the liberalism of Newman, had done just the opposite. "I say that the English reliance on our religious organizations and on their ideas of human perfection just as they stand, is like our reliance on freedom, on muscular Christianity, on population, on coal, on wealth—mere belief in machinery, and unfruitful." Now Arnold came down against games and sports except as a means to an end and a somewhat limited one at that—"a better and sounder physical type for the future to work with," for: "Culture does not set itself against games and sports; it congratulates the future and hopes that it will make good use of its improved physical basis; but it points out that our passing generation of boys and young men is, meantime, sacrificed." All that Arnold thought was necessary or desirable for the young, certainly for the sons of the working class, was gymnastics, arguing that if boys had to work long hours, or if they worked hard, gymnastics would do more for their physical health in the comparatively short time allotted to recreation than anything else would do.[4] The exaggeration of the games cult by the middle classes and their followers in other ranks of society had obscured for Arnold the possibility that participation in at least some sports might, in other circumstances, increase spiritual activity, increase sweetness, increase light, increase life, increase sympathy.

Victorian mountaineers, owing something to the stimulation of John Ruskin, did not subscribe to Arnold's view of their sport as mere machinery to which they were being sacrificed for physical benefits to future generations; they had early in the century abandoned the pretext that they climbed mountains for scientific investigations and believed that the dangerous and exhausting ascents of the lonely snow-covered Alpine peaks did indeed increase their spiritual activity. John Ruskin wrote *Modern Painters* to advocate the claims of English landscape painting, Turner's in particular, but through his analysis in magnificent prose, of mountain scenery, he opened the eyes of many of his fellow countrymen to the nobility of their Alpine journeys and, although he himself never ascended a peak of any magnitude, was elected a member of the Alpine Club shortly after its foundation in 1857.

Even as "machinery" sport had its advocates as well as its detractors. The products which were most commonly attributed to this particular machinery were physical health, moral character and military valour. Herbert Spencer, a scientist of renown, wrote an essay on "physical education" in 1859 in which he particularly castigated the current education of girls for its lack of physical exercise and recreation. Sport was conducive to health and "all breaches of the laws of health are physical sins."[5]

There was one piece of machinery which was certainly directly related to urban hygiene and which made possible the development of one particular sport. It was the swimming-bath. In the early part of the century epidemics of cholera had ravaged the growing towns and stimulated a widespread concern for better hygiene. The work and propaganda of Edwin Chadwick, one of the Poor Law Commissioners, and of other pioneers, prepared the way for the Public Health Acts of 1848 and 1875 and the Baths and Washhouses Act

1846. The health-conscious elected municipal bodies of the 1870s built swimming-baths to go with their washing-baths. Without these buildings many of which are still in daily use, swimming whether as recreation or competitive sport could not have been widely taken up.

Charles Kingsley in *Health and Education*, 1874, transferred the argument from hygiene to character-training—

> ... that games conduce, not merely to physical but to moral health; that in the playing field boys acquire virtues which no books can give them; not merely daring and endurance, but, better still, temper, self restraint, fairness, honour, unenvious approbation of another's success, and all that "give and take" of life which stand a man in such good stead when he goes forth into the world, and without which, indeed, his success is always maimed and partial.[6]

The association between sport and character-training was certainly taken for granted at Public Schools whence came the game of association football. The code of gentlemanly conduct was enforced as rigidly as the laws of the game. So long as the code was generally understood it was not even necessary to have a referee. When it became necessary to enlarge the rules of the game to cover accidental infringements or misbehaviour which could not be immediately foreseen, at first umpires and then a referee were empowered to control the game by a clause penalizing "ungentlemanly conduct." The clause is still retained in the laws of the game as a signpost to the morality of sport.

At the beginning of Chapter VI the connexion in Germany between sport and militarism was noticed. It might be thought that the development of competitive sport in England, even if it was regarded as machinery for hygiene or character-training, had few military connexions. Certainly the disasters of the Crimean War and the Indian Mutiny did not lead to increased playing fields but to the organization of Volunteer

Corps in Public Schools and the introduction of military drill in elementary schools. Nevertheless, there was a feeling—voiced in *Tom Brown's Schooldays* and in the statement about the Battle of Waterloo and Eton's playing fields, falsely attributed to the Duke of Wellington—that games did foster those qualities of physical courage, team loyalty and endurance which were certainly as valuable on the battlefield a; knowledge of the techniques of manœuvre and weapon-training. In Public Schools, training in the volunteer corps was never taken as seriously as training in games. "Play up, play up and play the game" was a cry that linked the playing- and the battlefield in the minds of many beside Henry Newbolt.

There were those who argued that the machinery of games and sports produced effects which were far from beneficial. Wilkie Collins in his novel *Man and Wife* maintained through the mouth of Sir Patrick Lundie that the essential principle of rowing and racing was to take every advantage of another man which superior strength or superior cunning could suggest so that the athlete "must go down (gentleman as he is) step by step . . . from the beginning in ignorance to the end in crime." The surgeon in the book could similarly say—

> From my own experience I can tell you that a proportion and by not any means a small one of the young men who are now putting themselves into violent athletic tests of strength and their endurance, are taking that course to the serious and permanent injury of their own health.[7]

As military training, too, games and sports had their critics. In Kipling's *Stalky and Co*, Stalky, McTurk and Beetle sneered at their school fellows because they played cricket and said "Yes, sir" and "No, sir." They themselves joined the natural history society in order to escape from school and their exploits usually ended with a thrashing. Yet at the end of the book the reader is asked to "imagine Stalky let loose on the south side of Europe with a sufficiency of Sikhs and a reasonable prospect of loot. Consider it quietly." Cricket was obviously not the best training machine for this kind of warfare.

Athleticism was strongest and most vigorous at the turn of the century and during the Edwardian era. Throughout the period of development the fundamental question whether sport was liberal in Newman's sense or machinery in Matthew Arnold's was never resolved, but most of those who played felt no great compulsion to find a justification for their games other than the satisfaction that they derived from their performance.

BIBLIOGRAPHY

1. MOLYNEUX, D. D., The Development of Physical Recreation in the Birmingham District 1871–1892, unpublished thesis, University of Birmingham (1957).

2. MOLYNEUX, D. D., op. cit.

3. ARNOLD, MATHEW, Culture and Anarchy, Chap. 1 (London, 1869).

4. TAUNTON COMMISSION Report of the Schools Inquiry Commission, Vol. VI, pp. 589–60 (1868).

5. SPENCER, HERBERT, Education, Intellectual, Moral and Physical (1859, 1891 ed., p. 170).

6. KINGSLEY, CHARLES, Health and Education p. 86 (London, 1874).

7. COLLINS, WILKIE, Man and Wife, p. 178 (1870 ed., London, 1902).

See also

ENSOR, R. C. K., England 1870–1914 (Oxford, 1936).

MACK, E. C., Public Schools and British Opinion from 1860 (New York, 1941).

NEWMAN, J. H., The Idea of a University (1851) (Everyman edition).

VIII

EXPORT

THE panorama of world sport in the middle of the twentieth century shows games and sports from many different countries of origin, judo from the Far East, polo from Asia, lacrosse from America, pelota from Spain, cycling from France, ski-ing from Scandinavia. Nevertheless, the majority of sports in current practice, and the very great majority of the more popular, were exported from Britain. They were taken abroad as soon as they were sufficiently refined and well organized to stand the journey and as soon as ambassadors, official and unofficial, colonial administrators, missionaries, merchants, soldiers, sailors and settlers took a mind to playing games in their new homes, whether these homes were temporary or permanent. The Scots in exile showed a particularly strong inclination to form Caledonian Societies and to play golf.

Golf, which was already well organized under aristocratic patronage in Britain during the eighteenth century, appeared in the United States three years after the Declaration of Independence in 1776. An advertisement in a New York paper of 21st April, 1779, read: "To the Golf Players. The season for this pleasant and healthy Exercise now advancing. Gentlemen may be furnished with excellent Clubs and the veritable Caledonian Balls by inquiring at the Printers." The export was here clearly labelled with the country of origin.

Similarly cricket, which had an accepted code of rules by 1744, was taken far and wide by colonists and others. A match in New York took place as early as 1751. The British Ambassador in Paris planned a game in 1789. Political events prevented stumps being pitched. Cricket was played by British soldiers at Lisbon in 1810 and by "the secretariat" during the Congress of Vienna. There was a cricket club in Calcutta before the end of the eighteenth century.

These early exports were not intended for foreign consumption and did not attract the people of the countries where they were introduced. Cricket made little impact in America, Asia or Europe in the eighteenth century, and golf, after its first notice in America, was not recorded again for about a century. It was in the second half of the nineteenth century that the export of games and sports reached significant proportions. Golf and cricket were but two on a list of many sports that had been organized at home and were enjoyed and practised by those who travelled abroad.

There seem to have been but few attempts to foist British games on native peoples as a deliberate move in colonizing large parts of the world. Doubtless some missionaries and some colonists introduced football to parts of Africa as curates and industrialists had done to parts of Birmingham and Liverpool. Lord Harris, too, when governor of Bombay actively encouraged the Indians to play cricket which they did readily and with skill; it is improbable that he used cricket consciously as an instrument of colonial policy. It is also difficult to believe that the British engineers who built the railway from Roskilde to Copengagen in the 1860s introduced cricket in order to Anglicize the Danes or even to further their commercial enterprise. Cricket was being played in many different European centres from Odessa to Christiania (Oslo) by British visitors and residents between 1880 and 1890. The game had only a slight following from Europeans. The same must be said of citizens of the United States which were visited in 1859 by the first professional touring team ever to leave Britain. It was in the British Empire and Commonwealth that cricket found its devotees. British troops introduced the game to South Africa in the 1840s. The British West Indies had a cricket club by 1842, while in Australia, Sydney, Hobart, Melbourne, Perth and Adelaide were all centres of cricket before 1850. After a visit by an English team in 1861–2 which drew crowds of twenty-five thousand to their matches, English professional coaches were engaged and cricket took firm root in Australia.

The United States rejected cricket but adopted another English game, baseball, and made it very firmly its own. Indeed, in 1908 the Spalding Commission which had been set up to inquire into the origin of baseball reported first that baseball was a distinctly American sport and had no connexion with "rounders" or any other foreign game; secondly that the first rules for playing baseball were devised by Abner Doubleday in Cooperstown, N.Y., in 1839. In 1939 a Hall of Fame was opened in Cooperstown to celebrate the centenary of this event. Alas, in that very year Robert W. Henderson of New York Public Library began to publish data which contradicted this theory. Both the name and the game baseball were known in England in the eighteenth century. The essential features and rules of the game were published in London in 1828 in *The Boys' Own Book*. Other evidence suggested that it was most improbable that Abner Doubleday could have been in Cooperstown in 1839. Whatever its origin baseball developed steadily after 1845. The rules were agreed. A National Association of Baseball Players, a strictly amateur body, was formed in 1858. In 1865 and 1866 professionalism made its appearance. In 1871 the National Association of Baseball Players was organized in New York and effective control of the game passed from the hands of amateurs to the promoters and professionals. The great growth in popularity with its attendant problems of professionalism and control of the game came in the decades following 1870.

Football was another game which was exported to the

United States and was Americanized although no attempt was made to obscure its origin. It appeared in two forms, the association and the Rugby games, soon after their formalization in England. Football had not been unknown in earlier centuries. John Wheelwright, a Cambridge friend of Oliver Cromwell and a keen footballer, went out to Massachusetts Bay Colony as a clergyman. From that time onward spontaneous games of kick and rush were played. The first refined game came, as in England, from schools and colleges which attempted to codify and unify the laws about 1871. Then in 1873 a team of Old Etonians arrived to play a team from Yale University under rules similar to those which had been adopted by the F.A. Two years later Harvard suggested to Yale that they might play matches and adopt the Rugby code which was already known in Canada. The suggestion was accepted and the game became popular at the two universities and thereafter at other schools and colleges. In 1876 the intercollegiate Football Association adopted the Rugby rules. The Rugby game, however, quickly took on American characteristics and although it became popular in the sense that it attracted huge crowds of spectators it remained primarily a college and high school game.

Between the end of the American Civil War and the turn of the century there was great development of sport in the States at first along the eastern seaboard and then elsewhere. Lawn tennis which had been patented in England by Major Wingfield in 1871 was taken to the United States from Bermuda in 1874. The first American championships were held in 1881, under English rules, and in the same year the American Lawn Tennis Association was formed.

The development of sport in America was haphazard if vigorous and in 1888 American athletes were provoked by the irregular and even chaotic condition of sport to found the Amateur Athletic Union. The Union claimed jurisdiction not only over track and field athletics but also over other amateur sports as they arose. The most important of these new sports was basket ball, invented by James Naismith at the Y.M.C.A. Training School, Springfield, in 1891, and popularized by the Y.M.C.A.s throughout the United States, and after 1900 throughout the world.

The growth of popular sport in the United States was parallel to that in Britain and during the nineteenth century similar steps in organization were taken some ten to twenty years after they had been taken in Britain. Probably the social and economic conditions which had determined the development of sport in Britain at mid-century did not begin to obtain in the United States, even in industrial areas, until after the civil war ended in 1865. On the European continent the spread of games and sports occurred later still. Germany was the first European country to adopt the Philistine sports of Britain—

> Very often English consular and diplomatic representatives, business-men or students resident in Germany, personally introduced their favourite sports in the locality where they happened to be staying, and were leading members of German sports clubs. English sporting expressions were taken over wholesale. Cries of "Foul" and "Offside" echoed across German meadows. In Berlin the fashion went so far that notices of forthcoming sports contests were printed in English.[1]

Sport came to Sweden by a process of proselytizing in reverse. In the 1870s Colonel Victor G. Balck began touring Europe with teams of Swedish gymnasts with the object of publicizing and popularizing Swedish gymnastics. In 1880 he visited Britain and was so impressed with the games and sports which he saw there that he determined to foster them in Sweden. The first modern athletic championships were held the same year and in the following year Balck started a sports periodical. The social conditions in Sweden were ripe for sport. Very quickly games and sports spread from the military training grounds to the country at large. Table II shows the dates at which sports associations were founded in Germany, Sweden, Britain, and the U.S.A. In Denmark the development was parallel to Sweden.

TABLE II

Years in which National Sports Associations Were Founded

	GERMANY	U.S.A.	SWEDEN	BRITAIN
Association Football	1900	—	1904	1863
Swimming	1887	1878	1904	1869
Cycling	1884	1880	1900	1878
Rowing	1883	1872	1904	1879
Skating	1888	1888	1904	1879
Athletics	1898	1888	1895	1880
Lawn Tennis	1902	1881	1906	1886
Ski-ing	1904	1904	1908	1903

In other European countries the introduction of English sports was more haphazard. Football reached Hungary, for instance, in 1896 through the medium of a young graduate from Cambridge, Mr. Arthur Yolland, who went to Budapest to teach English to the sons of the aristocracy at the Franz Joseph Institute. In the following year he began teaching them football. The Budapest Torna Club was founded and by 1900 football had taken root in central Europe. Indeed, by the turn of the century there was not a country in Europe which had not sampled British sport in one form or another.

If Britain was the source and origin of nineteenth- and twentieth-century sport the ways in which games were organized by the importers differed fundamentally. This was inevitable. The Philistine institutions which were closely associated with athleticism in Britain were copied only spasmodically and imperfectly elsewhere. Moreover, the organization of sport in Britain was essentially individual and even parochial. It was not to be expected that the two schismatic governing bodies of football would have much to do with each other, but it was surprising that none of the other governing bodies had anything to do with each other. Almost the sole point of contact among amateur bodies was amateurism. Most of them ruled that a performer who was declared a professional by another governing body would be regarded as a professional by themselves. As each body defined amateurism in a different way this individualism led in time to injustice and absurdity.

In the United States, when baseball and football had been lost to commercial and professional interests, the Amateur Athletic Union set up in 1888 took steps to control and to standardize the government of all amateur sports. In Sweden and Denmark in 1896 and 1903 respectively national sports federations were formed to co-ordinate the various branches of sport and to draw up common rules for the conduct of amateur sport.

In both Britain and in the United States industrialism brought leisure to the people. It also put money in their pockets. More and more people were prepared to pay to watch attractive games, and when they paid they expected play to be of a high standard. Gate money led naturally to professional performers and to the promotion of some games as commercial entertainments. Some British sports had known professionals long before the popularization of sport. Golf, horse-racing, cricket, pedestrianism and pugilism had all had their paid performers since the mid-eighteenth century. There was money to be made, too, by the backers and promoters. Nevertheless, the sports with their professionals and their commercial element were firmly controlled by an aristocracy who often made money from sport but who could also afford to lose money and frequently did so. This is something which the professional cannot afford and which the twentieth-century amateur has found increasingly difficult to do, with a consequent obscurity of the distinction between the two categories. However that may be, when professionalism and commercialism developed on a large scale in the nineteenth century the governing bodies succeeded, after some heart-searching, in keeping these elements firmly in their place. The place was not always the same in each sport but in no sport, except perhaps boxing and wrestling, was there widespread suspicion of corruption or the subservience of the sporting spirit to the commercial interest. At no time did commercialism of sport creep into Public Schools or Colleges, from many of which the sons of tradesmen were carefully excluded.

A very different set-up quickly appeared in intercollegiate competitions in the United States. Football-playing became a half-time occupation. Individuals were enticed into universities for their physical prowess and some of them made no serious attempt to study. The games were often attended by rowdyism and a number of universities from 1885 onwards banned football from time to time. Gate receipts, however, were a steady and lucrative source of income for colleges and enabled them not merely to offer athletic scholarships and to pay generous salaries to coaches, but also to erect costly buildings for sport and other activities. The commercial interest spread to the high schools, and interschool athletics was often financed from gate receipts. The National Collegiate Association did much to check the worst abuses of inter-collegiate sport, but college football continued to be essentially a professional game and, outside college, baseball was dominated by professional and commercial interests. The United States had neither the inhibitions nor the aristocratic tradition of control which enabled commercial sport in Britain to be kept within bounds.

The export of British games and sports was not universally welcomed abroad. Within the British Empire there was little if any opposition. The colonists and white settlers were glad to have a link with the homeland and this link was strengthened when a programme of international matches was begun, first in cricket and then in Rugby football and other sports. In the United States Anglophobia did not prevent the adoption of British games and sports. The pioneering spirit of the New World showed a readiness to sample any sport and then to adopt it, to remould it, or to reject it according to circumstances. Games and sports, however, formed an obvious bond between immigrants of different nationalities, different social backgrounds and even different languages. For a while the Germans held somewhat aloof in the sporting world in their own gymnastic societies, but even for them, by the end of the nineteenth century, sport was one of those factors which brought them into the American way of life.

In Germany itself the import of games and sports stimulated a vigorous and often acrimonious rivalry between the devotees of the indigenous sport of gymnastics, *Turnen*, and the advocates of the new sports. There was a tremendous upsurge of enthusiasm for physical recreation at the end of the century. The *Deutsche Turnerschaft* itself increased its membership from 170,315 in 1880 to 1,263,573 in 1914. By that time, too, there were another one and a quarter million members of other sports associations. The conflict between the two sports movements was not superficial, but reached down to fundamental beliefs on the role of sport in life and society. The *Turnbewegung* was a highly organized and centralized movement and certainly politically conscious. Since the 1848 risings the movement had been liberal in outlook and dedicated to the ideal of a free and united Fatherland. The sports movement on the other hand was of foreign origin; British in fact, spontaneous in its growth and devoid of leaders or political philosophy. Just because the movement was one of sport for sports sake it aroused the fierce opposition of the *Turners* who denounced it for its lack of higher ideals. To them the new sports smacked of materialism, hedonism and commercialism and until 1908 the *Turnerschaft* refused to support or take part in the Olympic Games. The striving for victory and for records and for public approbation was in the eyes of the *Turners* a perversion of effort. Until the First World War the Olympic Movement in Germany progressed in the face of opposition and criticism from gymnasts.

In Denmark and Sweden a somewhat similar situation led to a different outcome. The gymnastic movements in those countries had been a deliberate response to defeat and demoralization in the Napoleonic Wars and had, therefore been political and even military in character at the beginning of the nineteenth century. When the invasion of Sweden by sport took place in 1880 it was Victor Balck, a gymnast who later became Director of the Central Gymnastic Institute, who was seen to be leading the invading army. The other leaders of the gymnastic movement then began to think out afresh the fundamental tenets of their own movement and adapted and expounded their gymnastics to meet new needs and new tastes in recreation. Gymnastics became a part of the sports movement. It was not always well integrated but at least the gymnastic association joined the national sports federation.

Throughout the second half of the nineteenth century the export of games and sports from Britain took place without conscious direction from the governing bodies and with scanty interest from sportsmen themselves. Cricket was perhaps an exception because the Australians had shown in 1878 that they could cross the oceans and beat an English cricket eleven handsomely even when it included the great W. G. Grace. Generally speaking, however, the British showed a remarkable lack of interest in their sporting exports. The

G

greatest exporting operation of all was carried out by a Frenchman.

Baron de Coubertin, born in 1863, was obsessed in his youth, like so many of his compatriots, by the defeat of France in the Franco-Prussion war of 1871. Defeat often stimulates a concern for the training and education of the rising generations and de Coubertin was at an early age convinced of the need for reform in French education. While himself a schoolboy he read a French translation of *Tom Brown's Schooldays* (*Années de collège de Tom Brown* published by Hachette, 1874) and often subsequently referred with respect and sympathy to this educational novel. At the age of twenty he visited England and made his pilgrimage to Rugby School. From that moment he appears to have become an Anglophil of great persuasive power. *Tom Brown's Schooldays* as a novel gave by no means an accurate picture of Dr. Arnold and his views on sport but it did offer in 1857 the first exposition of the Public Schools' philosophy of sport and it was this that appealed to de Coubertin.

The Baron's first efforts for sport in France were directed to the infusion of sport into schools and *lycées*. In 1888 he had another idea. "L'Allemagne avait exhumé ce qui restait d'Olympie: pourquoi la France ne réussirait-elle pas à en reconstituer les splendeurs?"[2] He prepared the ground, now in England, now in the United States, and in November, 1892, at a meeting in the Sorbonne, he expounded his idea for the revival of the Olympic Games. In June, 1894, a Congress for the re-establishment of the Olympic Games was held in the Sorbonne. Seventy-nine delegates from fourteen nations and forty-nine organizations assembled and unanimously resolved to revive the Olympic Games. Was it significant that de Coubertin omitted to invite a German representative? He gave his own philosophy of sport at the dinner which closed the congress—

The Greek inheritance is so vast that all those who have studied physical education in one or other of its manifold aspects may with justice refer back to the Greeks who understood them all. For some, training was to defend the fatherland, for others the quest for physical beauty and health in an easy equilibrium of mind and body, that healthful tingling of the blood which some have thought the real joy of living, and which is nowhere so intensely and so exquisitely felt as in the exercise of the body.

All this was assumed at Olympia but with something in addition that since the Middle Ages no one has dared to put into words, because over physical qualities has hung a veil of reticence, isolating them from the qualities of the mind. Latterly, the physical has been allowed to follow in the steps of the spiritual, but always like an inferior who has been made to feel his dependence and his inferiority.

It is impossible to estimate the scientific and social consequence of this enormous error. In the last resort, man is not composed of two parts, body and soul, but of three; body, mind and character; it is not the mind that forms the character, but principally the body. The Ancients understood this, but our fathers forgot it and we are painfully relearning it.[2]

It is doubtful whether de Coubertin was interpreting correctly the philosophy of the ancient world or any part of it but he was certainly under the influence of the ethos of British Public Schools if not of Tom Brown himself for whom the training of character was the supreme value in sport. He was also moved by a desire to promote international friendship through athletic rivalry and wanted as wide a catchment as possible for the Olympic Games. However, in fairness to the Baron, we must record that he did not say "the important thing in the Olympic Games is not so much winning as taking part in them." This statement, so often attributed to de Coubertin, came from the Bishop of Pennsylvania preaching in St. Paul's Cathedral at the time of the Olympic Games in 1908.

Significant for the future of the Olympic Games and of

much international sport was the establishment and constitution of the International Olympic Committee decided upon by the Congress of 1894. It consisted of twelve members, one from each of the following countries: Greece, Russia, Bohemia, Sweden, New Zealand, United States, Hungary, Italy, Great Britain, Uruguay, and two from France. The committee was to recruit its own members from countries having national Olympic Committees and the members were to be elected for life. It was to be the final arbiter in all matters concerning the Olympic movement. This committee, so strangely constituted and endowed with such power from birth, made no pretence to be democratic. It had much more affinity to the eighteenth-century clubs which governed sports in Britain, the Royal and Ancient Golf Club, the Marylebone Cricket Club and the Jockey Club, than to the associations which had been founded on democratic principles in the nineteenth century to govern football, athletics, swimming and other emerging sports.

In one way the I.O.C. proved to be more British even than Baron de Coubertin for he had always envisaged the Olympic Games as a festival of individual sports—athletics, gymnastics, combat sports, water sports and equestrian sports. The I.O.C. from the beginning included a team game, football, in the programme and later introduced others such as hockey and basketball.

At its outset, then, the Olympic Movement looked back to ancient Greece for its ideal of physical prowess and the ennoblement of man in athletic contest. It looked to Britain and to Britain's Public Schools for a modern interpretation of the ancient ideals and it looked to Britain, too, for its organizational structure. These compliments were graciously received in Britain and at early celebrations of the Games the country was represented by those whom the chairman of the British Olympic Council described as "a few athletes who saw fit to take upon themselves the onerous duty of representing their country in international athletics." The export of sport was not yet taken seriously in Britain. Participation in international sporting events was haphazard and only after the twentieth century was some years old was any importance and prestige attached to winning international contests.

BIBLIOGRAPHY

1. DIXON, J. G., Prussia, Politics and Physical Education, in *Landmarks in the History of Physical Education*, ed. P. C. McIntosh (London, 1957).
2. SENAY, A. and HERVET, R., *Monsieur de Coubertin*, trans. K. MacGowan, (Paris, 1956).

See also

Encyclopaedia Britannica—articles on specific games and sports.
GREEN, G., *Soccer: The World Game* (London, 1953).

PART II · TODAY

IX

ATTITUDES TO SPORT IN THE TWENTIETH-CENTURY

By the beginning of the twentieth century sport was well on the way to becoming a world-wide and an international phenomenon. It will not be possible in considering sport during this century to keep every country and every development in view, but just because sport has become international, many of the developments and many of the problems and issues that have arisen in Britain have their counterparts elsewhere. It is not possible to be entirely insular either in theorizing about sport or in practising it. Glances across the English Channel, across the Atlantic and to the more remote countries of the world are becoming more and more necessary if the examination of sport in this country is to be well informed. In the remainder of this study, therefore, Britain will be taken as the focal point, but reference will be made to events and ideas abroad. In the final chapter some international implications of sport for all countries will be considered. The purpose of this next chapter, however, is to show how strains of thought and traditional practice from Britain's past have carried on into her sport in the twentieth century.

During the first forty years of the century the pattern of

sport which had been set by 1900 persisted with minor rather than major changes. The athleticism which had appalled Matthew Arnold, excited the contempt of later writers also. T. S. Eliot, for instance, in his *Notes towards the Definition of Culture* gave sport scant recognition. "Culture," he wrote, "includes all the characteristic activities and interests of a people: Derby Day, Henley Regatta, Cowes, the twelfth of August, a cup final, the dog races, the pin table, the dartboard, Wensleydale cheese, boiled cabbage cut into sections, beetroot in vinegar, nineteenth-century Gothic churches and the music of Elgar."[1] This statement, as Raymond Williams pointed out, marked a departure from Eliot's previously adopted meaning for *culture* as a whole way of life. It represented no more than "popular" culture, sport, food and a little art.[2] The very association of activities and interests listed by Eliot accorded sport a lowly place in any scale of cultural values. His estimation of sport was much nearer to that of Matthew Arnold as "mere machinery" than to J. H. Newman's "liberal pursuit." By 1948 when Eliot wrote his *Notes* sport was indeed becoming popular, not perhaps in Eliot's sense nor yet in Arnold's sense of pertaining to the Populace as distinct from the Philistines or Barbarians. It was popular in the sense that it pertained to the whole people and because of its universality was showing itself capable of bridging gaps between Populace, Philistine and Barbarian, between religious groups, between racial groups and between many other divisions of society.

It was still possible, however, in the 1950s for writers on culture to ignore sport altogether as a cultural phenomenon. F. R. Cowell wrote in *Culture in Private and Public Life*—

Some people, including many primitive tribes, are very much alive in an animal sense, but their primitive interests are so small that they seem relatively negligible ... Culture whether it took the form of music, song, dance, designing, painting, carving, reading or writing, would add a new interest to what may be shortly described as their basic or "animal" interests of eating, drinking, sleeping, keeping warm and dry, hunting and fishing and all other activities of a predominately routine and mainly biological existence.[3]

Into which category was sport to be placed? Cowell did not say. Dance was unequivocally cultural but sport was so difficult to award a cultural status and yet so ill-suited to a category of mere "biological existence" that it was ignored. Yet Cowell wrote later: "Culture owes its interest to its power of bringing meanings and values into life. The quest for culture, therefore, is the search for meaning and value." Was sport, then, unlike dance, devoid of power to bring meaning and value into life? If so it could hardly be neutral but must surely act as an opiate which dulled the senses, or at best was some outlet which satisfied some animal instincts during youthful years until maturity was reached and it could be safely discarded like a pair of outgrown football boots.

It is difficult to explain the omission of sport from many examinations and analyses of contemporary "culture." The explanation can hardly lie in a lack of interest in the relationship of body to mind for that interest is as keen as it has ever been, nor is it possible to be blind to the attention and energy, time and money that are devoted to sport by so many people. Perhaps the use of the word *culture* itself discourages a critical analysis of sport, for culture has never, except in a botanical or biological sense, taken happily to the epithet *physical*. Physical culture suggests Sandowism, exhibitionism, strength for strength's sake, and an unhealthy obsession with muscular and physical development which is the enemy of the full development of aesthetic and intellectual power. Furthermore, the acceptance of a dualist metaphysic and a sharp separation of body from mind has often led to a concentration upon things of the mind at the expense of bodily activities. Yet a neglect or denigration of physical activity and sport are not inevitable consequences of dualism. D. H. Lawrence took a liberal view of physical recreation and sport and certainly did not abandon his dualistic metaphysic in order to do so, far from it—

> If our consciousness is dual, and active in duality; if our human activity is of two incomparable sorts, why try to make a mushy oneness of it? The *rapport* between the mental consciousness and the affective or physical consciousness is always a polarity of contradictions. The two are never one save in their incomprehensible duality. Leave the two modes of activity separate. What connexion is necessary will be effected spontaneously.[4]

And again he wrote: "if you are going to be physically active, physically strenuous and conscious, then put off your mental attention, and become a mindless physical spontaneous consciousness." Yet he was anxious to accord to this physical self-expression a worth and a dignity which it had seldom received in the past.

The body was not an instrument, but a living organism, and true physical self-expression could never be "mere machinery." Athleticism and Swedish drill were anathemata to him, but the exercise of physical skill in conquering the elements, in contest sports and above all in combat sports was an expression of man's innate nature which could dignify and complete his life. What disturbed Lawrence was that his society had not seen that sport was essentially competitive and that work, productive work, was non-competitive. The spirit of contest had been introduced into all spheres of life, commercial, industrial, spiritual, educational and even religious. Men had to a great extent abandoned honest contest and instead had made all work a scramble of contest against some other worker. Sport and work should be separately conceived and executed in different ways, competitive and non-competitive. Within the gymnasium—and Lawrence was in favour of the gymnasium—he wanted "fierce, unrelenting honourable contest." The gymnasium should fulfil the same purpose that it did for the Greeks; "the purpose of pure perilous delight in contest and profound mystic delight in unified motion." He restated, too, the Greek conception of pain and agony in training and contest. "Where there is no pain of effort there is a wretched drossy degeneration, like the hateful cluttered sheep of our lush pastures." By contrast with the pasture-fed sheep the wild sheep was "a fleet, fierce thing, leaping and swift like the sun" and Lawrence's admiration of "spontaneous, mindless animation, in motion sheer and superb, like a leaping fish, or a hovering hawk or a deer which bounds away" was reminiscent of Wordsworth's child of nature who—

> . . . shall be sportive as the fawn
> That wild with glee across the lawn
> Or up the mountain spring . . .

Lawrence was specific about sport in his long essay on "The Education of the People" but he worked out his ideas from time to time in his novels *The Rainbow*, *Women in Love*, and *Sons and Lovers*.

All too many aspects of sport in the 1920s failed to reach the ideals of physical consciousness which Lawrence set for it but they did not prevent his pointing towards the mystic and intrinsic value which competitive sport could have.

Bertrand Russell was one of those who abandoned a dualist philosophy and who saw a value in physical activity as a result of adopting a monist position. In *Education and the Social Order* he argued that class distinctions gave a greater prestige to the care of the mind than to care of the body and that because children's academic education was carried out separately from their physical education and by separate people, there was for adults a gulf between mind and body which was "not a metaphysical necessity but a product of education." If the two tasks of training the mind and training the body were combined in one teacher all children "would grow up to be neutral monists, believing that mind and matter are only different aspects of the same phenomenon."[5]

The "aspect" theory was developed by a number of Russell's followers. They argued that the ultimate furniture of the world was neither mental nor physical, but events of a neutral kind that could be ordered in different ways. Russell once stated that mind and matter, like the lion and the unicorn fighting for the crown, were simply heraldic inventions. The neutral monists and their descendants the logical positivists may not have set out to rehabilitate sport, but they certainly took up a position where the battle between body and mind, a battle in which the body had so often been worsted, was irrelevant.

The twentieth century has been characterized by many fundamental re-examinations of the relationship of body and mind. There are perhaps four main groups of theory current today. First there are the interactionists who maintain as they have done from the time of Hippocrates and of Galen that bodily events affect mental events and mental events bodily ones. Secondly, some scientists seek the ultimate explanation of human behaviour in terms of neurological, physiological, biochemical or electromechanical events. A third group consisting mainly of clinical psychologists pin their hopes of explaining human behaviour in answers to psychological questions yet to be formulated. The last group of theorists regards questions about body and mind as waste of time and seeks, instead, to improve methods of observing and describing human behaviour.[6] There has, too, been a close look at the very nature of causality. Such re-examination and three of the four current theories listed above allow and even encourage new thoughts about the nature of physical activity and sport as a social and individual phenomenon. In the past the image of sport and physical recreation has suffered because the "body" has been a natural target on which to project the frustrations of disease, discomfort, pain, lack of power and human inertia. The investigations of the neurophysiologist, and the chemist have revealed how unfair many of these strictures on the body have been and have given the body a new dignity which pertains to its voluntary as well as to its involuntary activities.

Popular attitudes change more slowly than the sciences or systems of philosophy and one continuing feature of sport in Britain in the twentieth century is Puritanism. More than anywhere else Puritanism left its mark on the English Sunday. G. M. Trevelyan quotes a German visitor to London in 1710—

> In the afternoon to St. James's Park, to see the crowds. No other diversion is allowed on Sunday, which is nowhere more strictly kept; not only is all play forbidden, and public houses closed, but few even of the boats and hackney coaches may ply. Our hostess would not even allow the strangers to play the viol di Gamba or the flute lest she be punished.

Trevelyan says that the visitor added that Sunday observance was the only visible sign that the English were Christians at all.[7]

More than two hundred years later in 1924 the Olympic Games were held in Paris. The heats for the one hundred metres fell on a Sunday and Eric Liddell, one of the British competitors with a very good chance of winning the event, refused to run for reasons of conscience. Fortunately a compatriot, Harold Abrahams, was still able to win the gold medal for Britain. Fortunately, too, the four hundred metres heats and final were arranged on week-days and Eric Liddell was able to win that event.

Eric Liddell's protest was a spectacular but not isolated manifestation of the Puritan view of the Sabbath. Until 1960 Rule 25 of the Football Association read as follows—

> Matches shall not be played on Sundays within the jurisdiction of this Association. A player shall not be compelled to play on

Sundays outside the jurisdiction of this Association. A Club or player shall not be compelled to play any match on Good Friday or Christmas Day. A person who takes part in Sunday Football in the United Kingdom shall not be recognized by this Association.

In May 1960 the Football Association at its annual general meeting decided to recognize Sunday football and County Associations were thereafter allowed to invite Sunday Leagues and Clubs to affiliate. However, no club or player could be compelled to play on a Sunday and it remained illegal by the law of the land to charge gate money for a game on Sunday. The Sunday Observance Acts had long made this a crime and the Lord's Day Observance Socity had been vigilant to uphold the law. In 1961 the Society forced an action in the courts against the promoters of a match on a Sunday to raise funds to aid spastics. The action was won.

The Wolfenden Committee, whose report *Sport and the Community* was published in 1960, gave "considerable thought to this delicate and difficult subject [Sunday Games]." After saying "we cannot . . . join forces with those who wish to impose on the general public their own interpretation of keeping the Lord's Day holy" the report then laid down four principles on which this very thing might be done. The Committee disapproved of the idea of organized sporting meetings on Sundays. The implication of their remarks was essentially Puritan. It was wrong to make or take money on Sunday. Sunday games should not coincide with morning services in church. Those who refused to play on Sunday should not be excluded by their clubs from games on weekdays and Sunday games ought not to make unnecessary work for others by their demands for accommodation, the preparation of pitches and the provision of equipment.

This last negation is highly significant. Most of the indoor facilities for games and sports in Britain are part of or attached to schools. Some are to be found in buildings owned by private clubs and some are provided by voluntary organizations such as the Y.M.C.A. or Y.W.C.A. There are, too, public swimming-baths and other municipal facilities. Private clubs are open to their members on Sundays but all school premises and indoor sports facilities under the Y.M.C.A. and Y.W.C.A. are bolted and barred, while municipal facilities are available to a limited extent.

This lack of availability is only partly due to religious conviction. There are important considerations of labour and maintenance which are difficult to face. However that may be, the lack of availability of indoor premises and even grass pitches has encouraged the great outdoor movement associated with canoeing, sailing, climbing, potholing and simply walking which has been such a marked feature of the mid-twentieth century. The hills and the rivers are open on Sundays. The closure of facilities for sport on Sundays within the urban areas is difficult to reconcile with demands for additional facilities for sport, particularly when these demands are supported by the argument that such facilities would have a beneficial effect upon the incidence of crime and juvenile delinquency. If there is an inverse relationship between sport and juvenile delinquency—and this has yet to be proved—it might be argued that existing facilities might make a larger contribution to the reduction of delinquency; not only on Sunday but also on week-days if they were not put out of use on one day in seven by a rigid sabbatarianism enforced by convention and law.

Sabbatarianism is in the Puritan tradition but is by no means the only manifestation of that tradition in sport. Puritanism and Puritans have worked for as well as against sport. Many bishops and clergy of all denominations have taken a keen interest in sport in this century as in the last, and the inclusion of a bishop, who had in earlier days been a rowing blue, in the Committee under Sir John Wolfenden in 1960 excited no

DESCRIPTION OF THE PLATES

Plate 1

Elizabeth Ferris. Participation in competitive sport has been a marked feature of female emancipation in the twentieth century. In style events such as diving and skating women have reached a peak of performance essentially their own and they command admiration equal and perhaps superior to that of their male counterparts.

Plate 2

The stadium at Delphi (2a) was the site of the Pythian Games. These games, together with the Games at Olympia, Nemea and Corinth, were the four recognized Panhellenic festivals. Runners raced up and down and spectators stood on the terraces. By the second century A.D. top-level sport in the Roman world was commercialized and highly organized. The structure of the *Flavian amphitheatre at Rome* (Colosseum) (2b) still shows the domination of sport, if sport it was, by spectators.

Plate 3

The first modern Olympic Games in 1896 were held in *a reconstructed stadium of ancient Greece in Athens* (3a). The shape did not appeal either to the competitors or spectators and stadia of the twentieth century conform to the pattern of the Roman world which enables the maximum number of spectators to view a handful of performers. *Wembley Stadium* (3b) is typical but by no means the largest modern stadium.

Plate 4

Hackney Marsh. Local authorities in Britain provide facilities for sport for large numbers who will never attract spectators and could not afford to provide their own facilities. On Hackney Marsh the London County Council has laid out 111 soccer, rugger and hockey pitches superimposed on 3,000,000 cubic yards of rubble from London buildings which were bombed in the 1939–45 war.

Continued on page 105

2a

2b

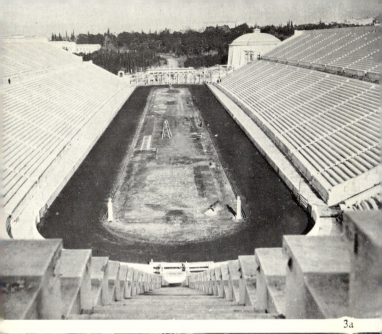

3a

3b

5b

6b

7a

7b

DESCRIPTION OF THE PLATES

Plates 5 and 6

Propelling the body uphill is an intrinsic part of some sports, as in the *Three Peaks Race in Yorkshire* (6a). Skiers, however, increasingly regard going uphill as a chore to be performed by machinery. Even *Cairngorm in Scotland* (5a), for many years patronized only by the energetic up-hill walker, now has a ski-lift. Maximum exercise with minimum skill still makes its appeal but an increasing number of people are seeking maximum skill for the minimum expenditure of energy. Mechanization has enable *the golfer Dwight D. Eisenhower* (5b), President of the United States 1952-60, and many other sportsmen to achieve this objective. In some sports a machine or a force outside the human body provides the actual challenge for the use of skill. The waves rolling on to the *beach of Tamarana at Sydney* (6b), and on many other shores provide just such a challenge for the surfer.

Plate 7

Sport for the elderly and for the disabled. Fishing on a Scottish loch (7a) with a boatman is a sport confined to a few but sport for the elderly is having increasing attention from sporting bodies. Sport for the paraplegics *at Stoke Mandeville Hospital for spinal injuries* (7b) is no longer merely therapy but is a form of self-realization for the injured no less than for the able-bodied. Sport for the disabled has now attained the level of international matches, one of which is shown here.

special comment. Puritanism, however, has had a more subtle influence on sport than that which has been exerted by the direct interest of churches and ministers of religion. The great acceleration of athleticism and the growth of competitive games in the nineteenth century, with their supposed potential for training character, was an intrinsic part of the intensely competitive commercial development and imperial expansion of that era. These features of Victorianism owed much to Puritanism as R. H. Tawney showed so brilliantly in *Religion and the Rise of Capitalism*—

> Puritanism was the schoolmaster of the English middle classes. It heightened their virtues, sanctified, without eradicating, their convenient vices and gave them an inexpugnable assurance that, behind virtues and vices alike, stood the majestic and inexorable laws of an omnipotent Providence, without whose foreknowledge not a hammer could beat upon the forge, not a figure could be added to the ledger. But it is a strange school which does not teach more than one lesson . . . the heart of man holds mysteries of contradiction which live in vigorous incompatibility together. When the shrivelled tissues lie in our hand, the spiritual bond still eludes us.
>
> In every human soul there is a socialist and an individualist, an authoritarian and a fanatic for liberty, as in each there is a Catholic and a Protestant. The same is true of the mass movements in which men marshal themselves for common action. There was in Puritanism an element that was conservative and traditionalist, and an element which was revolutionary; a collectivism which grasped at an iron discipline, and an individualism which spurned the savourless mess of human ordinances; a sober prudence which would garner the fruits of this world, and a divine recklessness which would make all things new.[8]

So wrote Tawney in describing "A Godly Discipline versus the Religion of Trade." His words illuminate the apparent conflict between contempt for sport, because there must not be idle leisure and "those that are prodigal of their time despise their own souls," and the encouragement of sport and devotion to it at schools and colleges of religious foundation, Catholic, Protestant and Nonconformist alike. In those institutions, sport was harnessed to the training of character, self-discipline and the tolerance of pain, discomfort and danger whether in the scrum or on the bumpy wicket. The Puritan, "tempered by self-examination, self-discipline, self-control, is the practical ascetic whose victories are won not in the cloister, but on the battlefield, in the counting house, and in the market." One might add "and on the playing-field but not on Sunday."

The indecisiveness about whether sport contained its own justification within itself or whether its value was to be sought in ulterior ends was revealed in Acts of Parliament, in debates in both Houses of Parliament and other public pronouncements about sport. The Education Act of 1918 allowed local education authorities to provide camps, centres for physical training, playing-fields and swimming-baths and "other facilities for social and physical training." The wording of the final phrase suggested a strictly utilitarian attitude to sporting facilities. Similarly, when in 1935 the Central Council of Recreative Physical Training was set up by teachers and local government officers concerned with physical education, the title containing the word *training* emphasized the idea of improvement and discipline rather than unalloyed enjoyment. It is true that the word was softened by the qualification *recreative*. Less harsh in concept was the National Playing Fields Association formed in 1926 and associated with an appeal "for the financial help of every citizen who recognizes the need for a greater co-operative effort to give our young people a chance to play the game and not merely to continue as onlookers." Here at last was public recognition of the need and the right to play for play's sake. Nevertheless, when in 1937 the government decided to give financial and legislative support to physical recreation and presented the Physical

Training and Recreation Bill to Parliament Oliver Stanley
who moved the second reading, after mentioning the recreative purpose of the scheme, went on to stress the training and
therapeutic side of the Bill. He claimed that wise and scientific
training given under proper instruction could do much to
remedy some of those minor and, indeed, major ills to which
a highly civilized and industrialized society was liable. The
government clearly felt that they could subsidize sport only
on the basis of preventing "the idle use of leisure."

The Puritan origin of government policy was revealed and
denounced in the debate by Aneurin Bevan—

> I think [he said] the desire to play is a justification in itself for
> playing; there is no need to seek the justification of national well-
> being for playing, because your own well-being is a sufficient
> justification. The idea that you must borrow some justification for
> playing is one of the worst legacies of the Puritan Revolution.

He went on to accuse the government of pushing physical
training on the masses because it was easier and cheaper than
providing the facilities and playing fields which the upper
and middle class enjoyed—

> This idea that you must get all the boys and girls in rows, like
> chocolate soldiers, and make them go through evolutions, is a
> miserable substitute for giving them sufficient playgrounds in
> which they can play their own games in their own ways.

When allowances have been made for the polemics of
political controversy there are still two issues of social significance revealed in the debate. The Populace, despite its devotion
to the terraces of the football grounds and its own games on
the commons and in the parks, was well aware that it did not
enjoy the opportunities and facilities for sport which were
available to the middle class, let alone the aristocracy. Aneurin
Bevan was resisting the imposition on the Populace of
recreation which was different in kind from that enjoyed by
more favoured classes. Gymnastics and physical training,

especially when done in the mass, had a long association with the playgrounds of the Board Schools, elementary schools and the military training of "other ranks." They had, therefore, a flavour of social and political lack of privilege which they did not have in any other country. The question raised was whether this Bill was a measure designed to perpetuate in recreation and sport a class structure and an educational system which was already felt to be ready for overhaul.

The second issue was whether physical recreation and sport, or more particularly the expenditure of public funds upon them, could be justified except for the non-sporting benefits which would accrue. The promoters of the Bill and many of its supporters in Parliament clearly thought in terms of payment by results even if they were asking for payment in advance. At least one Member of Parliament associated the Bill with the current rearmament programme and regarded it as a measure to promote premilitary training. Health, fitness and social morality were the other expected results. Aneurin Bevan called himself a heretic because he advocated the abandonment of physical training for ulterior ends in favour of play for its own sake. He was thinking of political and educational heresy but he was in fact raising an issue of long-standing religious and metaphysical import which was certainly not settled in the British House of Commons in July, 1937.

Parliament voted £2,000,000 and the government set up a National Fitness Council under Lord Aberdare to promote the objects of the Act. The name itself signified that Aneurin Bevan had not won his point. The World War, however, which began in the late summer of 1939 had two very different effects upon sport. On the one hand it stimulated a campaign of "fitness for service" so that men and women inside and outside the armed forces took vigorous exercise with the deliberate aim of preparing themselves for rigours known and unknown; on the other it stimulated a concern for the rising generation which was essentially liberal in character. The Education Act of 1944 was worked out and passed through Parliament at the height of hostilities. It looked far into the future and envisaged a much wider spread of educational privilege. It also made the provision of facilities for sport obligatory on Local Education Authorities. Although the new Ministry of Education which now replaced the old Board of Education still looked at sport between educational blinkers of physical training and recreation, the general trend was to make available for the children of the Populace the kind of facility which had long been enjoyed by Public Schoolboys and girls.

The National Fitness Council was a war casualty not much lamented. In January, 1944 the Central Council of Recreative Physical Training significantly changed its name to Central Council of Physical Recreation. This marked a major break-away from the idea of doing good to the people and a step towards giving to the people what they wanted in the way of sport and recreation. It also marked a move towards the breakdown of social barriers within the world of sport. While soccer, cricket, swimming, athletics, boxing and lawn tennis were national sports in that they had keen adherents among all classes, cycling, wrestling, weight-lifting and coarse fishing were largely confined to the so-called working-class. Fencing, badminton, hockey, lacrosse, women's cricket, squash rackets, rackets, fives, horse-riding, sailing, ski-ing, mountaineering and sail-plane gliding were middle- and upper-class sports. So, too, were golf except in Scotland and Rugby football except in Cornwall and South Wales and in the Rugby League in Yorkshire and Lancashire.

The work of the Central Council of Physical Recreation in spreading sport widely through the land was made possible by a state of full employment and by an increase in spending power among younger adults. Yet the different social origins and traditions of different sports continued to reveal themselves in unexpected ways. The Philistine revolution of sport discussed in Chapters VI and VII was a middle-class revolution. The Philistine form of organization for sport was different from that developed by the aristocracy earlier. The latter had exercised authority through the "club." Clubs were not primarily sporting organizations. The club as an institution dates back, at least to 1659, but became distinctly an upper-class institution at the end of the eighteenth century. They were exclusive and confined to "gentlemen." Often they were named after the proprietor of premises where they met. White's founded in 1698, Boodle's in 1762 and Brooks' in 1764 were three of the best known. The aristocracy used the same form of organization for controlling their sports and in cricket the same nomenclature. The cricket ground opened by Mr. Thomas Lord in 1787 and patronized by the Marylebone Cricket Club became known as Lord's. The Jockey Club controlled horse-racing, and the Royal and Ancient Golf Club controlled golf. Perhaps the last club to be founded which controlled or exercised a controlling influence over a sport was the Alpine Club founded in 1857 and recognized by mountaineers as a centre of authority. The Amateur Athletic Club founded in 1866 failed to exercise authority and had to give way to an association in 1880, the Amateur Athletic Association, which was not socially exclusive and whose general committee was democratically elected. From the foundation of the Football Association in 1863 onwards the democratic association was the form of government adopted for and by the many different sports which developed.

Nevertheless, the sports governed by clubs never quite lost their aristocratic connexion and the sports governed by associations never quite gained full aristocratic status. The great Public Schools, Eton, Winchester, Westminster, might continue to patronize soccer and the monarch might attend the cup final of the Football Association, as King George V did in April 1914, and appear to give that sport the stamp of royal approval, yet in 1953 the first knighthoods ever to be given for performance in sport, as distinct from administrative service, went to a cricketer, Jack Hobbs, and a jockey, Gordon Richards. The conquerors of Everest, too, received knighthoods. No more than a C.B.E. was awarded to the first man to run a mile in less than four minutes and when, in 1957, the name of the pre-eminent player of association football for twenty-five years appeared in the New Year's honours list it was seen that he too was to rank no higher than Commander of the Order of the British Empire. A headline in the *Daily Mail*, "So it's not Sir Stan after all," expressed the keen and widespread disappointment of the Populace that Stanley Matthews and his sport, soccer, had not been counted worthy to receive the Queen's accolade.

If social distinctions within sport were slow to die, so was parochialism. British sport had been inward-looking and the governing bodies of sport had been set up to organize their respective sports for those who had a well-defined interest in them. They were not recruiting boards or coaching organizations nor was any one of them more than mildly interested in what the many other governing bodies did. The great achievement of the C.C.P.R. was to provide for all of them a servicing organization offering propaganda, training and technical advice. Swimming had had a teacher-training scheme since 1899 and soccer since 1934 but by 1944 this was almost the limit of organized coaching in Britain. The expansion of coaching and the provision of far more opportunities for more people in more sports after 1944 was greatly aided by the work of the C.C.P.R. and its technical officers. The C.C.P.R. was less successful in breaking down parochialism in sport. Although all governing bodies of sport became constituent members of the C.C.P.R. they retained their autonomy and their isolation from each other. Subjects of common concern were rarely sought out and discussed. A policy for British sport was never evolved, certainly not a financial policy.

The Central Council itself was grant-aided by the Ministry of Education in respect of its educational work, but many of its activities were financed by the participants or from voluntary funds. Complaints were often heard in post-war years that the government gave no aid to sport. They became more frequent as news came from abroad that other governments were giving generous help to sport and sports organizations. The governing bodies in Britain neither severally nor in concert through their Central Council asked the government for aid except within the narrow educational terms of the grants for social and physical training. In the nineteenth century fear of "pauperizing" the poor, that was making them physically, socially and morally dependent on the rates or on public funds, stood in the way of many government welfare projects. Similar fears lay beneath the reluctance of those who controlled sport to ask for money from public funds. There was also a genuine fear of state interference with sport and leisure. This fear was succinctly expressed by the guest of honour at a dinner to inaugurate a fund which would pay the expenses of representatives to the Olympic Games in Melbourne in 1956. In response to a question about state aid he expressed the view that Britain did not wish to send a team of temporary civil servants.

The condition and the position of sport as a whole in Britain never underwent serious examination until 1956 when the Department of Physical Education at the University of Birmingham produced a survey and an analysis of British sport in a booklet *Britain in the World of Sport*, and drew attention to technical problems, finance, international implications and to philosophical issues. Among its modest achievements the publication stimulated the C.C.P.R. to set up in 1957 a Committee already mentioned under the chairmanship of Sir John Wolfenden "to examine the factors affecting the development of games, sports and outdoor activities in the United Kingdom and to make recommendations to the Central Council of Physical Recreation as to any practical measures which should be taken by statutory or voluntary bodies in order that these activities may play their full part in promoting the general welfare of the community."

In these terms of reference Aneurin Bevan's old heresy reappeared. Sport was "to play a part in promoting" a purpose further off. There was a reluctance to recognize that the purpose of sport was within sport itself. However, whatever the terms of reference were, the introductory chapter to the report of the Committee which appeared three years later, did advance the proposition that sport was self-justified. It also recognized the effects that sport might have for instance upon the development of qualities of character valuable to individuals and to society, upon the social behaviour of citizens, upon the promotion of health—although the Committee did not accept that there was a causal link here—and upon aesthetic experience. The Committee came nearest to stating a strictly utilitarian view of sport in dealing with juvenile delinquency. It reported—

> The causes of criminal behaviour are complex, and we are not suggesting that it would disappear if there were more tennis courts or running tracks; nor are we concerned to press for wider provision of opportunities for playing games just on the ground that it would reduce the incidence of those various forms of anti-social activities which are lumped together as "juvenile deliquency." At the same time, it is a reasonable assumption that if more young people had opportunities for playing games fewer of them would develop criminal habits.[9]

The assumption was reasonable certainly, but unproven, and as if suddenly seeing the yawning abyss of utilitarianism the writer quickly turned round and wrote on—

> But our major thesis is that there is a positive "play" element in the life of young people, which can be neglected only to the disadvantage of both individual and society.

> Man in short, needs play. In the form of a game, a sport or an outdoor activity of some kind it is desirable in itself, for its own sake, as a valuable element in a full and rounded life.

Is this view either acceptable or accepted in the modern world? The following chapters attempt to give a tentative answer.

BIBLIOGRAPHY

1. ELIOT, T. S., *Notes Towards the Definition of Culture*, p. 31 (London, 1948)
2. WILLIAMS, R., *Culture and Society*, p. 230 (Penguin Books, 1961).
3. COWELL, F. R., *Culture in Private and Public Life*, p. 4. (London, 1959).
4. LAWRENCE, D. H., Education of the People, in *Phoenix* (London, 1936).
5. RUSSELL, BERTRAND, *Education and the Social Order*, pp. 151–3 (London, 1951).
6. REEVES, I. W., *Body and Mind in Western Thought* (Penguin Books, 1958).
7. TREVELYAN, G. M., *English Social History*, p. 328 (London, 1944).
8. TAWNEY, R. H., *Religion and the Rise of Capitalism*, Chap. 4 (ii) (London, 1926).
9. WOLFENDEN COMMITTEE, *Sport and the Community*, pub. Central Council of Physical Recreation (London, 1960).

See also

PHYSICAL EDUCATION ASSOCIATION OF GREAT BRITAIN AND NORTHERN IRELAND, *Britain in the World of Sport* (London, 1956).

Parliamentary Debates on Physical Training and Recreation Bill, July, 1937, in *Hansard* (London, H.M.S.O.).

X

THEORIES OF WHY AND HOW

SPORT has always flourished in civilized societies even when the environment has not been favourable. Under the Roman Empire the professional athletes, tightly organized in their guilds and unions, converted the great stadia from Nîmes to Antioch into "closed shops," yet informal play and sport still persisted at a lower level. When monasticism thrust a repressive asceticism upon Christendom sport remained a solace and a joy to villagers and townsmen and even, on occasion, to monks. Calvinism and Puritanism in their extreme forms were unable to prevent ordinary people from committing the sin of indulging in sport. While the people played, philosophers and educationists examined the contribution that physical activities and training might make to the development of society and of the individual. Until the twentieth century, however, few attempts were made to examine why people played or how sportsmen achieved their results. Only recently has the phenomenon of sport and sporting performance been analysed by social scientists, physiologists, psychologists, physicists and mathematicians.

Some of the first investigations were concerned with play itself. The fact that animals, children and grown-ups all play excited the interest of researchers. Numerous and various attempts were made to define or describe the biological function of play. The discharge of superfluous vital energy, abreaction—an outlet for harmful impulses—wish-fulfilment, satisfaction of the imitative instinct, a form of training for the more serious side of life, satisfaction of an innate urge to dominate, these roles were ascribed to play as a feature of human existence. In so far as sport is playful the roles could also be transferred to it as an individual and social phenomenon. All these psychological or biological theories of play made a fundamental assumption that play was a means to an end, that it had some biological purpose, and was ultimately determined by something that was not play. In the past, many, indeed most, philosophers and educationists had justified sport as a means to an end and few had seen it as self-justified, so now biologists and psychologists were making a similar assumption about play. J. Huizinga in the 1930s pointed to the fact that all such theories could only offer partial solutions to the problems which they set out to solve, because they left almost untouched the questions what play was in itself and what it meant for the player. In a book entitled *Homo Ludens* he set out to answer these questions and "to show that genuine, pure play is one of the main bases of civilization."[1]

Huizinga's concept of play was succinct. He recognized that not every language could have hit on the same concept and found a single word for it. He took, therefore, the concept corresponding to the English word *play* and defined it as follows—

> play is a voluntary activity or occupation executed within fixed limits of time and place according to rules freely accepted but absolutely binding, having its aim in itself and accompanied by a feeling of tension, joy and the consciousness that it is "different" from "ordinary life."

Huizinga claimed that this definition embraced play in animals, children and grown-ups, games of strength and skill, inventing-games, guessing-games, games of chance as well as exhibitions and performances of all kinds. It would also embrace dancing, even in its free forms and such non-competitive sports as hunting, and sports of adventure such as climbing, and crossing the Atlantic alone in a thirteen-ton yacht. When the etymology of the English word play is considered its relevance to adventurous sports is even more obvious. *Play* comes from the Anglo-Saxon noun *plega*, or verb *plegan*. The oldest meaning of these words is "to vouch or stand guarantee for, to take a risk, to expose oneself to danger for someone or something." The words *pledge* and *plight* are both etymologically connected with *play*.

Huizinga did not identify play with sport nor did he say that play was an essential element in sport by definition. He did maintain that play was a valuable ingredient in sport, so valuable that when sport lost this particular element it became divorced from culture and had little dignity or worth for mankind. The precise relationship of play to sport is a matter for argument but a closer examination of Huizinga's definition of play shows how much is lost from sport if play is extinguished or obscured.

Huizinga's definition lays down three conditions which apply to play. First is freedom. The player cannot be forced to participate without the activity changing its nature. To run round a track by command of military or civil authority in order to prove a certain degree of attainment or fitness causes the act of running to be no longer play. Compulsory games at school are only play when the intrinsic interest and challenge so dominate the players that the original obligation is forgotten. For a number of boys and girls this never happens. The particular activity may then be valuable as a form of physical education, but it is not play. The contempt of some adults for sport has undoubtedly originated in the extinction of the play element in their physical education in childhood and adolescence.

The second condition is separateness. According to Huizinga the activity must be circumscribed with boundaries of time and space that are precise and fixed in advance. Such circumscription certainly applies to all competitive games and sports. The running track, the cricket pitch, the fencing piste, the slalom course, the chess-board all prescribe the area of play. The time factor is known to the competitors in advance. But what of some of the non-competitive sports, angling, mountaineering, hunting? The prescription of time and space is very indefinite and may be changed by those who take part during the course of their activity. In these sports the physical environment itself, the river or loch, the peak, the habitat of the quarry provide the limitations which in other sports have to be imposed by definitions of time and space.

The third condition is regulation, and this is more fundamental than the other two conditions. Conventions and rules of a sport suspend the ordinary rules of life and for the duration of the sport the new law is the only one which counts. Even the play of animals appears to be regulated by certain self-imposed regulations eliminating serious injury or death. In the sports of human beings the degree and complexity of regulation varies. It might be thought to be least complex in the play and the sports of children and most complex in the sports of adults. This is not necessarily so. Hopscotch is much more carefully regulated than mob football, which has been played for centuries by adults. However, the purpose of the regulations is to define the sphere in which the ordinary rules of life are suspended, to define the unreality of the sport. They also help to define the nature of the skill to be employed or the way in which chance may operate. Limitation to provide scope for skill is very well exemplified in the off-side laws of team ball-games. There is no rule which has done more to transform violent and brutish sports into games of grace and skill. As recently as 1829 it was recorded that a Frenchman passing through Derby and seeing a game of football remarked that if Englishmen called this playing it would be impossible to say what they would call fighting. Football and other games have undergone some refinement since then and there is now hardly one team ball-game which does not work under an off-side regulation. Even basket-ball, which for many years was played without such a rule, now has the so-called "three-second" rule which prevents a player waiting under the opponents' basket to receive a pass and put the ball in. In games of skill the regulations strictly limit the areas for the operation of chance, strength and skill. They also provide artificial obstacles for the exercise of skill and thereby enable players to obtain an utterly useless but definite result. In a sport such as mountaineering the environment provides the regulation, yet artificial regulation is sometimes wanted in addition in order to preserve the play element. In the 1930s in Britain there were sharp differences of opinion on the justification for using pitons on English rock cliffs, and again in the 1950s disputes arose whether it would be legitimate to use mortars to dislodge snow and ice during an ascent of Mount Everest. Even in mountaineering, then, regulation or convention is necessary for the separation and differentiation of sport from ordinary life.

In amplification of his definition of play Huizinga notes that society is more lenient to the cheat than to the spoil-sports for the spoil-sport shatters the play world itself. He robs play of its illusion, i.e. *in-lusio*.

Modern pharmaceutical research has led to a problem of cheating which is only superficially scientific but in reality philosophical. In the Olympic Games of 1960 the Danish cyclist Knud Jensen collapsed during the one-hundred-kilometer race and died later. It was established that he had taken a drug, Ronicol, which has the general effect of stimulating the circulation by dilating the blood-vessels. The effect of the drug, the exertion of a big race and the heat of the day combined to kill him. In the next year Toni Hiebeler and his three companions made the first winter ascent of the North Face of the Eiger. Hiebeler and his companions also used Ronicol to stave off frost-bite. The use of the drug may well have saved their lives as well as enabled them to reach the summit. Death or glory has always been the ultimate alternative in mountaineering and in some other sports and is not incompatible with the fundamental concept of sport or with the play element in sport. Death, of course, immediately shatters the illusion of unreality and if death or glory is the inevitable as well as the ultimate alternative as it was in many gladiatorial combats in ancient Rome then indeed the combat is neither play nor sport.

The use of drugs in sport can be questioned philosophically but not medically. It would only destroy the basis of sport if it broke the conventions or regulations defining the area of unreality, and to decide such an issue is difficult. Regulations are deliberately framed and specific; conventions, which are sometimes more important than the rules, are often unconsciously accepted and are non-specific. Malice, anger and loss of temper are generally thought to destroy sport, but where mechanical aids are concerned convention is capricious. In athletics starting-blocks and spiked shoes have been accepted, but built-up heels for high jumpers have been rejected. In lacrosse the use of body protection in Canada and the United States and the rejection of it in England have led to the development of two essentially different games, neither one being less nor more a sport than the other.

Drugs have hitherto been thought of as unsporting because their effect was to impair performance and the only way to use them was to administer them to an opponent. Poor Abraham Wood inadvertently drank liquid laudanum received from pretended friends while he was contesting a pedestrian contest with Captain Barclay Allardice in 1807 and shortly afterwards had to resign the match. More recent products have been found to have positive rather than negative effects on performance and a different situation has, therefore, arisen. No serious attempt has yet been made to regulate the use of

I

drugs for positive assistance. Already caffeine is widely used by professional cyclists and Varidase was used by boxers in the Olympic Games in 1960 to minimize the effects of bruising. Other sportsmen take other drugs, some to stimulate, and some to relax or induce sleep between two strenuous efforts. Pharmaceutical research has been rapid and spectacular. The American Medical Association has estimated on the basis of research at Harvard that amphetamine alone could improve the performance of runners by one and a half per cent and swimmers by one per cent. As the use of drugs becomes more and more a part of daily life so the governing bodies of sport will need to decide how to regulate their use and still maintain a satisfactory and acceptable area of competition or play where the ordinary rules of life are suspended. Until that is done it is impossible to decide whether, in Huizinga's terminology, the taker of drugs is a cheat, a spoil-sport or neither.

The second part of Huizinga's book sheds light upon the manifestation of play in culture as a whole, in law, in literature, poetry and drama, in art and in war. This does not concern us here, but consideration of Huizinga's definition of play has already led us towards differentiating sports in order to understand their essence more fully. Three problems of relationship present themselves: the first lies between unorganized play and organized sport, the second between games of skill and games of chance, and the third between competitive and non-competitive sport. These problems arising from Huizinga's work have been tackled by Roger Caillois.[2] In order to clarify the problems and offer solutions to them he devised his own classification which is presented schematically in Table III.

The table shows a horizontal classification to deal with the problem of relationship between unorganized play and organized sport and a vertical classification to deal with the other two problems, that is to say the relationship between games of skill and games of chance and between competitive and non-competitive sport.

The horizontal classification attempts to deal with a problem which was left unsolved by Huizinga, namely how to account for the variation of the play element in different games and sports, and its variation within a single sport performed at

TABLE III

Caillois' Classification of Play

	AGON Competitions		ALEA Chance	MIMICRY Pretence	ILINX Vertigo
PAIDIA			Comptines	Childish	Children's
Noise	Races	⎫ not re-	Heads or	imitation	swings
Agitation	Combats	⎭ gulated	tails	Masks	Merry-go-
Laughter	Athletics			Costumes	round
Dance					Tetter-
Hoop	Boxing		Betting		totter
Solitaire	Fencing		Roulette	Theatre	Waltz
Games of	Football				Outdoor
patience	Checkers		Lotteries		sports
Crossword	Chess				Ski-ing
puzzles					Mountain-
LUDUS					climbing

different levels of competence. Huizinga ended his book with a sweeping condemnation of sport which is difficult to support. He maintained that in modern sport the old play factor had undergone almost complete atrophy. Increasing systematization and regimentation had led to the loss of the play quality and the neglect of playing for fun. The division between professional and amateur had led to a situation where the professionals were marked off as inferior in standing to true players but superior in capacity, a situation which had produced an inferiority complex in amateurs. "Between them they push sport further and further away from the play sphere proper until it becomes a thing *sui generis*: neither play nor earnest. In modern social life sport occupies a place alongside and apart from cultural process." Huizinga even added that sport no longer had any organic cultural process.

It might have been easier to accept Huizinga's analysis in 1938 than it is in 1963. It is easy to see the encroachment of the principle of commercial entertainment upon the sphere of playing for fun in professional sport at the highest level and even in some so-called amateur sport at the same level. The price which the best performers pay for success is the sacrifice of almost all, but not quite all, the spontaneity and play element. The winner of the British Open Golf Championship in 1961 and 1962, Arnold Palmer, claimed that in the final days of preparation for a big competition he must have complete freedom from care; that he must be free to play a round or not, and even abandon a round if he felt a lack of enthusiasm for it. Part of his recipe for success was to maintain a vestige of the play element right into the big competition.

Whatever may be said of the divorce of professional and commercial sport as entertainment from the concept of sport as play, it would be difficult to maintain in the 1960s that the part-timers in sport suffer an inferiority complex because of the superiority of the professionals any more than amateur dramatic performers or amateur musicians suffer from a psychological complex because of the existence of professional actors and musicians performing in commercial theatres or municipal concert halls. In the public parks, on the commons and village greens, in halls, squash courts and swimming-baths the play element is very much a feature of sport. Systematization and organization by themselves do not appear to destroy or undermine sport.

Caillois' graduation from *paidia* to *ludus* is an attempt to show a progressive formalization of play from the spontaneous activities of children to the organized play of adults. He does not thereby answer Huizinga's strictures on modern sport but he does suggest that formalization is not incompatible with playing for fun.

In his vertical classification Caillois distinguishes competitive sport (*agon*) from games of chance (*alea*), from play which is dramatic (mimicry) and from activities which seek the sensations of falling or centrifugal force, games in which "people have deliberately sought out the confusion that a slight giddiness provokes."

The distinction between games of skill and of chance is illuminating. The former "implies discipline and perseverance. It makes the champion rely solely on his own resources, encourages him to make the best possible use of them, and forces him to utilize them fairly and within fixed limits which, being the same for everyone, result in rendering the superiority of the winner indisputable." The latter, on the contrary, is "based on an inequality external to the player, over which he has not the slightest control . . . fate is the sole agent of victory, and where rivalry exists, victory means only that the winner was luckier than the loser." In short, a game of skill is a vindication of personal responsibility in an artificially contrived situation, a game of chance is a resignation of the will, a surrender to destiny also in an artificially contrived situation. This is true only of the two types of game in their extreme form. In bridge or poker reason and psychological insight are allowed to the player as a means of defence against the lot assigned to him by fate.

A comparable distinction can be seen within that group of activities which seek satisfaction in speed, giddiness, vertigo, or the subjection of the being to the risk of loss of equilibrium or to its actual loss. In the fairground switchback the abandonment is complete, but in the downhill ski run the exhilaration of speed and hazard is heightened by the awareness of skill and of power to control the forces of nature to a safe and successful completion of the run. In such a sport there is acceptance rather than abandonment of responsibility. Caillois' category of vertigo is thus seen not to be fundamental but to subdivide within his classification of competition and chance depending on whether resourcefulness or resignation is the dominant factor.

The vertical classification is least satisfactory in dealing with non-competitive sport. The predatory sports, hunting, shooting and fishing, are not mentioned at all, nor is swimming in its non-competitive form. Mountaineering and other similar outdoor sports appear in the category of "vertigo" as if the climber derived his satisfaction from a feeling of giddiness rather than from the exercise of skill. But vertigo may never be experienced during a climb which may still be intensely satisfying to the climber. Dancing, too, is unhappily divided between vertigo, which includes the waltz, and mimicry, which presumably includes various forms of expressive dance.

Close consideration of Caillois' category of competition (*agon*) shows that it is not wide enough. The essential feature of sport, as distinct from other realms in which the element of play is to be found—games of chance and dramatic or mimetic play—is the striving for superiority and this may take a personal or an impersonal form. The playful element in this striving means that victory is never complete and for all time and that defeat is never irreparable. The effort to conquer an opponent, the self or an environment in play and only in play gives to sport its peculiar satisfaction and its especial virtue in human life.

The desire for superiority in play is itself subdivisible. To prove oneself or one's team better than an opponent or an opposing team within prescribed limits is the aim and object of all competitive sport. The areas for the exercise of skill for the sportsman to prove himself or herself "better than" are many and variable. The running-track, the cricket field, the tennis court, the billiard table, the football pitch, the swimming-bath, the river estuary and many other locations allow sportsmen with different aptitudes and abilities either singly or in pairs or in larger groups or teams to strive for superiority in their chosen sphere of useless contest. These activities comprise a broad category of sport.

A second category comprises combat sports. Here again the aim of the contestant is to prove himself "better than" an opponent. The special feature of personal contact with the opponent either directly through limb and body or indirectly through foil, blade or single stick deserves a special category.

A third category might be called conquest sports. In these the challenge is provided not by an individual or group of opponents but by an environment or a situation. Mountaineering is the purest example of a conquest sport although on occasion even here the environment may be personified. It was reported that the comment of one of the party which made the first successful ascent of Mount Everest was "we knocked the bastard off." A more sensitive reaction to a successful climb was that of Mallory many years earlier. He lost his life on Everest in 1924. "Have we vanquished an enemy? None but ourselves. Have we gained success? That word means nothing here . . . We have achieved an ultimate satisfaction." For most of those who take up conquest sports the appeal is just the impersonal nature of the challenge. Swimming, cycling, hiking, camping and many other activities offer opportunities for conquest sports. Much educational gymnastics, which is non-competitive, makes its appeal as a conquest sport.

There is a fourth category of physical activity which is not sport but which needs to be considered here because of affinity with it. In this type of activity the object is not to be "better than" but to express or communicate ideas and feelings using and enjoying the movements and sensations of the body in the process. Dance, dance drama, eurhythmics and some systems of gymnastics such as those developed by Medau or Idla fall into this category.

The classification of sport here given depends on the motive and the nature of the satisfaction which the sport gives, not upon the activity itself. Swimming when it is not competitive may well be a conquest sport. The environment of water has to be conquered by the would-be swimmer. It may even become an expressive activity when it takes the form of synchronized swimming and is done to a musical accompaniment. On the other hand mountaineering on occasions becomes competitive and the first ascent of the Matterhorn by Whymper and his party with its tragic ending became just that. Even dancing may become a competitive sport when prizes are given for the best troupe or group in a dance festival. Some sports, even while remaining competitive, may make their appeal to a particular individual for aesthetic rather than competitive reasons but such an individual is unlikely to be successful in the toughest contests. An American high jumper once said to his inferior English opponent: "Sure I like your style but I prefer my height." Many players feel in the midst of their vigorous activity that they are expressing their personality. Indeed, all sport is expressive in this sense, yet in competitive sport it is nevertheless true that the dominant object is to be "better than." In sport and in dance human motives are never simple but it seems justifiable to postulate dominant desires and corresponding satisfactions.

There may well be a sex link with the classification given above, with women being attracted more by the fourth category of expressive activities and men more often deriving satisfaction from sports in the first two categories. There are

many good women games players and many men who are
excellent dancers, yet the vast following of women for "keep
fit" classes in Britain and for other similar systems of movement in other countries suggests that they find particular
satisfaction in release of tensions and expression of feeling
through rhythmical movement. Men on the other hand
clearly dominate numerically the playing fields of the world,
and more often derive satisfaction from proving their
superiority in a chosen sport.

An "adolescent growth study" carried out in California in
1947 shows just such a sexually divergent pattern of interest.
The study was carried out on adolescents by adolescents and
was designed to find out what qualities were most admired in
boys and girls of different ages. The most admired qualities
among boys of eleven to thirteen years of age were skill in
organized games, aggressiveness, boisterousness and unkempt-
ness. At the age of sixteen admiration for physical skills,
courage, strength and aggressiveness was retained, and even
later at the age of nineteen skill in competitive sport still had
prestige value.

On the other hand among girls success in games was
tolerated but not imitated. At the age of sixteen good sportsmanship with the implication of active participation in sport
was admired. At the age of nineteen athletic prowess carried
little prestige by itself but skill in dancing and swimming was
considered an advantage, so was skill in tennis, the competitive
game above all others in which boys and girls can meet each
other on common ground.[3]

Any society which is to provide a pattern of sport where
all its members may satisfy their natural desires must afford
opportunities in all categories. A feature of development in
Europe and America and Australasia since the end of the war
in 1945 has been the great increase of participation in conquest
sports, such as camping, canoeing, sailing, ski-ing. For some

the conquest sports become competitive after the basic skills have been mastered, but for very many the appeal of these sports remains impersonal for most of the time. The social significance of this growth of conquest sports is still obscure but some of its implications national and international will be examined in later chapters. There has also been a great increase in competitive sport both domestic and international at all levels from mediocre schoolboy football to first-class competition in the World Cup and the Olympic Games. This feature, too, will be examined in later chapters.

The "how" of sport has been investigated by so many researchers during the present century that it is only possible to notice in general terms two opposite approaches. In the first an interest in the problems of performance has shed light upon problems outside sport and has led to further investigations in other realms. The second approach, which is more common, has been from the opposite direction. Investigation of sport has been secondary to a primary interest in some other topic, such as disease or industrial techniques. An example of the first approach is the classical paper on "The Theory of Games of Strategy" presented by John von Neumann in 1928 to a mathematical congress. The paper was concerned with the following question—

> n players S_1, S_2 ... S_n are playing a given game of strategy G. How must one of the participants S_m play in order to achieve the most advantageous results?

A game of strategy, roulette, chess, baccarat, bridge, consists of a certain series of events each of which may have a finite number of distinct results. In some the outcome depends on chance, i.e. the probabilities with which each of the possible results will occur are known, but nobody can influence them. All other events depend on the free decision of the players. Von Neumann worked out a theorem on a system of constants which always satisfied three conditions expressed in the form of three equations. The theorem could only apply, however, to games of strategy where the free decisions of players could be implemented with precision as in draughts, bridge or chess. In games of strategy involving physical skill free decisions are but imperfectly implemented even by the most skilful players and the theorem is for them also imperfect.

In his final sentence von Neumann says: "In conclusion I would like to add that a later publication will contain numerical calculations of some well-known two-person games (poker, though with certain schematical simplifications and baccarat). The agreement of the results with the well-known rules of thumb of the games (e.g. proof of the necessity to bluff in poker) may be regarded as an empirical corroboration of the results of our theory." Von Neumann had at least satisfied himself that birds could fly.

Von Neumann's work stimulated a large number of mathematicians to analyse games of strategy. In 1959 the University of Princeton published four large volumes of such papers. The publication was sponsored by the Government's Office of Naval Research, not, presumably, because of the predilection of sailors for poker but because the analysis of games of strategy was seen to have an important bearing upon the conduct of warfare.

The movement of investigators in the opposite direction, from military to sporting activities, is exemplified by the programme of the Division of Human Physiology within the Medical Research Council of Great Britain. The Division was set up in 1949 under Dr. Edholm and within two years was investigating two paramilitary problems—the physical development of cadets at the Royal Military College, Sandhurst, and survival at sea. The first problem led to an examination of the sporting activities of the cadets as well as their military training. The second problem led to experiments on channel swimmers. Experience during the war had suggested that maximum time for survival in water at the temperature of the English channel was five to six hours, yet channel swimmers were known to be in the water for any time from twelve to twenty hours.

The next investigations had less connexion with military problems although they were relevant to a parapolitical problem of national prestige. They concerned problems of climbing at high altitude first on Eric Shipton's expedition in 1951–2 to explore the Southern approaches to Everest, then on the expedition which went to Cho Oyu and finally on the ascent of Everest itself in 1953.

In 1955 the Division began work on the study of whole-body-training using brief daily training sessions. It became interested in peak performance in sport and has had research workers at the Olympic and Commonwealth Games. There have been other research teams from other countries investigating the physiological problems of sport and the general trend in the west is an increasing interest in the intrinsic problem and a fading interest in military, political, or other utilitarian considerations. At the same time in the communist countries research into sport is tightly harnessed to political purposes. Perusal of the research reports of, for instance, the High School for Physical Education at Leipzig in Eastern Germany shows that many, if not all, of the research projects are chosen with political considerations in mind. In the United States a proportion of the thousands of research projects on physical performance have had little purpose other than to secure a higher degree for the research worker. Undoubtedly, however, the sum of research has made coaching sport more intelligent and more systematic. There is a risk that concentration on techniques and technical knowledge may obscure the element of play in sport, but the majority of those who play are not noticeably corrupted by being informed why and how they do what they do.

BIBLIOGRAPHY

1. HUIZINGA, J., *Homo Ludens*, p. 5 (1938, English ed., London, 1949).
2. CAILLOIS, R., The Structure and Classification of Games, in *Diogenes*, No. 12 (Winter, 1955).
3. FLEMING, C. M., *Adolescence* (London, 1948).

See also

COZENS, F. W. and STUMPF, F., *Sports in American Life* (Chicago, 1953).

HENDERSON, R., *Bat, Ball and Bishop* (New York, 1947).

NEUMANN, J. VON, *Theory of Games* (London, 1930).

RIESMAN, D., GLAZIER, N. and DENNEY, R., *The Lonely Crowd* (Princeton, 1950).

STOKES, A., Psycho-Analytic Reflections on the Development of Ball Games, *International Journal of Psychoanlysis*, Vol. XXXVI (1956).

XI

AFFLUENCE AND SPORT

THERE is money in sport. This proposition has been true for at least two and a half thousand years. About the year 594 B.C., according to Plutarch, Solon decreed that an Athenian victor in the Isthmian games should be paid 100 drachmae and an Olympic victor should receive 500 drachmae. An ox was then valued at 5 drachmae and these rewards for athletic prowess are seen to have been very generous indeed. No doubt long before 594 B.C. there had also been a commercial interest in selling sacrificial victims for the altar of Zeus, and in catering for the needs and whims of spectators and competitors. In Rome seven hundred years later under the empire a *ludus* in the Circus might involve twenty-four races a day for fifteen days. The organization of trainers, veterinary surgeons, grooms, jockeys and stable police was probably as intricate as it is today. There was a racing industry then as now.

Fencing and the teaching of fencing had their rewards in Tudor England. There was money in boxing and cudgelling when Tom Figg opened his combat school. The prize-ring, the race-course, the cockpit, the pedestrian contest all had a flourishing commercial side. There is nothing new in money being made by competitors, trainers, promoters and those who provide ancillary services to sport. With few exceptions the money to be made comes ultimately from the spectator. There is nothing new in this fact either. Euripides blamed spectators for the evils of athleticism in the fifth century B.C. However, it is not in every era that spectators have been organized to produce money for promoters of sports. Often the crowd has been a spontaneous gathering and the patronage

of a few rich men has provided the necessary financial backing
for a sport or sporting event. One rich man with £1,000 to
spend can be replaced by twenty-thousand with a shilling
each. The nineteenth century was the great age for the
organization of spectators and the commercial development
of sports on the basis of the shillings and pence of the poor.
When William MacGregor founded the Football League of
twelve clubs in 1888 his avowed aim was to provide regular
entertainment like that provided in the theatre. Professional
performers were engaged by the clubs to fulfil this aim. The
League was the culmination of commercialization lower down.
Aston Villa Football Club had taken no more than £43 in
gate money in 1878–9. Two years later the figure was £567
and by 1882–3 the annual report stated "so large are the sums
of money involved in the balance sheet that the club has
assumed the proportions of a large business affair." About the
same time (May, 1880) a Birmingham newspaper observed
"every little cricket and football club now considers it
necessary to hold its annual sports in order to benefit its
finances. The "gate" is of course the great attraction . . . "[1]
It was in the 1880s that sports which could command gates
from urban wage earners, notably football and cricket,
became industries and joined the ranks of sports already
commercialized if not industrialized, like horse-racing and
boxing. Other sports could command modest gates only.
Cycling and athletics were among them. Still others, such as
fencing and hockey, had almost no gate whatever. This
pattern remained substantially the same until the end of
World War II. Only the richest governing bodies, the F.A.,
the Rugby Union, the M.C.C. and the Lawn Tennis Association were able to pay salaries or expenses to the best players
and then plough back surplus money into their sports for the
benefit of ordinary clubs and players. The vast majority of
sportsmen paid for their sport themselves or depended on the

benevolence of local authorities, churches or charities for pitches and other facilities.

The two great commercial sporting enterprises of the nineteenth century, League Football and country cricket have survived into the second half of the twentieth century. The survival of county cricket is perhaps the more remarkable since the game goes on for three days at a time, week in week out during the summer. The total annual gates in the county championship dropped from their peak of 2,126,000 in 1949 to 1,641,000 in 1955 and continued their downward trend in following years. Throughout the hours of play on week-days the benches and stands in the county grounds yawn their emptiness at the players on the green. Three contributions have kept county cricket alive, the profits from Test Matches, football pools organized by the clubs, and such money-raising events as whist drives. In 1956 a Political and Economic Planning Report suggested that only two courses were open: to remove first-class cricket from the commercial sphere altogether and to rely primarily on membership as the non-competitive clubs do, or to organize cricket more fully as an entertainment and to rely more heavily on gate and ticket money. In either event full-time six-day professional cricket could not survive on any large scale. The report ended with these words: "Along with the English licensing laws, early closing, driving on the left and British weights and measures, it may survive and confound all its critics." Six years later in 1962 county cricket still survived in company with the other anachronisms listed.

League Football took a severe knock in the winter of 1961–2 when Accrington Stanley, one of the original clubs in MacGregor's league, founded in 1888, went into liquidation. In 1949–50 the estimated total attendances at football matches, association and Rugby, were 86,000,000 and gross receipts from clubs were £7,750,000. Allowing ten per cent for attendances at Rugby matches the figure of seventy to eighty million attendances at soccer matches compared favourably with five million for cricket, twelve million for speedway racing and fifty million for greyhound racing. The football league alone attracted about forty million spectators in the season. The total number of attendances dropped to about thirty-three and a half million in 1958-9 and to twenty-eight million in 1960-1. Many clubs in the third and fourth divisions of the League could no longer make ends meet with gate money but came to rely on substantial contributions from supporters' clubs. Neither television nor broadcasting fees made good the diminishing gate money. Like county cricket, League Football found that its financial foundations had been eaten away. A new structure had to be built which would house and provide employment for far fewer full-time professional players. In 1962 this fundamental and necessary reconstruction still waited for architect and builders to tackle it.

Both cricket and football in Britain are sports as well as entertainment industries, and they flourish. Despite a slight decline in the number of players of these two games between 1949 and 1960 the club game is still financially viable. Members' subscriptions, donations, bar receipts and other sources of income provide an adequate basis for continuing with existing facilities. Nevertheless, it is clear that in a society of increasing affluence cricket and football and other traditional team-games are not attracting the same proportion of people's spare cash nor are they giving the opportunities for promoters, manufacturers of sports goods and the providers of services to make money as once they did.

The changing pattern of sport in Britain and in the United States has naturally interested the bankers. Leisure is big business in the affluent society. In July, 1959 the Federal Reserve Bank of Philadelphia made a survey of twenty different sports in the United States in order to estimate the

K

number of participants and the money spent upon them. The general findings were that there were two hundred and eighty-six million participants and that the financial outlay by them was $8.3 billion. In addition they spent $10 billion indirectly on facilities, travel and such like. Some of the findings were more revealing—

1. Thirty-seven million people were active in boating in 1958 and spent $2 billion on their sport. Their number had doubled since 1954.

2. Thirty million people went fishing and twenty million went hunting and spent $3.6 billion.

3. Twenty million ten-pin bowlers spent $400 million. In 1946 there had been twelve million bowlers.

4. Four million golfers spent $750 million. In the 1920s golfers numbered about four hundred thousand.[2]

The social implications as distinct from the purely financial aspect of this new pattern of recreation will be discussed in later chapters. In England an article in *Lloyds Bank Review* in 1960 indicated similar trends in expenditure although the author was not able to give precise figures. He did, however, quote figures to show that the Golf Foundation Ltd., "a non-profit-making body supported by the industry" has induced no less than four hundred boys' and girls' schools to take training courses from professionals paid by the Foundation and has coached factory workers at over two hundred centres at 25s. for ten lessons. Angling, too, was a popular British sport and boasted about two million adherents. Hunting, too, increased its following after the war. In 1939 there were one hundred and seventy packs of hounds but by November, 1953 there were about one hundred and ninety in spite of the fact that to hunt a pack one day a week before the war cost £1,000 a season and £2,000 in 1953. The ordinary one-day-a-week follower in Leicestershire would spend £200 in a year provided that he rented no stable and looked after his own horse. Farmers, as distinct from gentry, had come back into hunting. In the north of England it was common practice among some factory workers and miners to work night-shifts so that they could go out on foot when hounds were meeting in their neighbourhood. There has been a very great increase in sailing in Britain. The first Boat Show at Olympia in 1953 attracted one hundred and twenty thousand visitors. In 1960 approximately two million five hundred thousand visitors came to see the products of three hundred exhibitors, fifty more exhibitors than in the previous year. In another sport, ski-ing, the trade reported an annual turnover of £2 million in ski equipment and the demand was rising each year. Clearly, then, opportunities for making money from sport and public taste in spending it are not dissimilar in Britain and in the United States.

Investigations of money spent on sports are paralleled by investigations into the spending power of different sections of the population. Adolescents in 1959 had considerable sums for free spending after paying for their board and income tax. Boys had 71s. 6d. per week and girls 54s. per week to spend. Although they represented no more than ten per cent of the population they accounted for far more than that percentage of all consumer-spending on, for instance, bicycles and motor-cycles, record-players, cigarettes and tobacco. Their expenditure on recreational goods and on holidays represented 18.2 per cent and 12.9 per cent respectively of all consumer-spending.[3]

The vast amounts of money spent on some sports and the large sums available to many individuals for free spending have prompted the question: "Can sport be entirely self-financing?" It has been argued that sports on the decline should be allowed to go their downward way and that we should not seek to secure the survival of one expensive sport after another by obtaining state grants or encouraging betting as a means of raising funds. One of the paradoxical consequences would be that the ability of the tax-payers to spend on the sports they enjoy would be decreased in order to subsidize those they did not enjoy.

At first sight this is a plausible argument, but if followed to its logical conclusion the result might be unwelcome. The sports which have shown a great increase in popularity since 1945 are outdoor recreations involving expenditure on personal equipment but making use of existing facilities, such as snow slopes, mountains, rivers, lakes, the sea, the countryside and golf courses. No expensive buildings, hard porous surfaces, well-drained turf—except on the golf courses—or heated and chlorinated water is required. Such sports can certainly be self-financing in the affluent society. All the necessary facilities exist already, but in general they are to be found outside, usually well outside urban areas. The *laissez-faire* doctrine would, therefore, tend to make travelling a necessary prelude to sport for most people living in towns and cities. Sport would then consume more of the leisure time which is rapidly becoming available.

The fact is, however, that even the sports of the hills, rivers and the lakes are finding the task of financing themselves increasingly difficult. In the United States the dwindling facilities for outdoor recreation led to the setting up of an Outdoor Recreation Resources Review Commission. After three years of study the Commission's recommendations led the President of the United States in 1962 to propose to Congress that a land conservation fund should be established to acquire land for recreation over the following eight years. Congress would be asked to authorize advance appropriations of $500 million.

The outdoor, non-urban sports fit in well with the tendency of young and old to spend money on personal possessions especially those which carry status. A car, a motor-cycle, a dinghy, a canoe, a bicycle, a rucksack, a climbing-rope are all personal and all carry status in one or another section of society. There is less inclination to invest personal incomes or savings in a joint enterprise such as a playing-field or a multi-sports centre. Furthermore, it is doubtful whether even in the affluent society the individuals who wish to participate in sports which involve heavy capital investment could organize their finances in such a way as to provide facilities. It is quite certain that adolescents have not the experience or the initiative, even if they have the money, to provide a swimming-bath, let alone a multi-sports centre. Both the Albemarle Committee Report on Youth Service and the Wolfenden Committee Report on Sport and the Community pointed out in 1960[4] that even under the existing arrangements of the Welfare State and the Affluent Society, the adolescent section of the population was starved of opportunities and facilities for sport.

The dimensions of the problem are these: in 1962 a standard school gymnasium which might provide either a single badminton court, or a substandard basket-ball court or a volley-ball court or facilities for judo, boxing, fencing, weight-lifting, but not, of course, all facilities at the same time, cost about £16,000 excluding the cost of the site. A swimming-bath large enough for competition and diving cost about £30,000, excluding the cost of the site. On the outskirts of London when in 1961 the local authorities wanted to develop forty acres of disused reservoirs and filter beds partly for schools and partly for a sailing and canoeing training centre for youth, they found that commercial developers were prepared to pay £2 million for the site. Land at £50,000 per acre would make sport on the doorstep a very expensive commodity for the town dweller if that sport were to be fully paid for by those who take part. In South London in the same year the site of the old Crystal Palace was already under the control of the L.C.C. and a multi-sports centre costing £2 million was being built there. At Cardiff the swimming-pool built for the Commonwealth Games in 1958 cost £750,000 and took £300 a day to keep open for ordinary use. Maximum takings from the public came to £200, leaving the remainder as a charge upon the rates. Sports which require no building, such as football or tennis, are only within the reach of the ordinary citizen because the site value of many of the central pitches and courts is ignored or obscured.

It seems inevitable that if sport were left to be self-financing without support from the central government, local authorities, the great charitable trusts or benevolent industrial firms, those which require buildings or land and all within the great conurbations would decline almost to the point of extinction. Is this a prospect which any modern society or any government of whatever party could, should or would be ready to accept?

Apart from the cost of facilities and of day-to-day participation in sport there are other financial burdens of modern sport which have to be shouldered. They are three: first, government and administration, second, coaching and third, the organization of local, national and international competition. How are these tasks carried out in Britain?

Coaching is a function shared by a number of statutory and voluntary bodies including the governing bodies of sport. The other two duties are performed solely by the governing bodies or by composite bodies such as the British Olympic Association to which the governing bodies remit some of their functions in the interests of co-ordination. The assets on the balance sheets of a selection of governing bodies gives some indication of their ability to shoulder their financial burdens.

ASSETS: 1959

	£
Football Association	397,859
Lawn Tennis Association	279,883
Rugby Football Union	238,430
Rugby League	87,059
Amateur Swimming Association	16,218
Amateur Athletic Association	12,567
All England Women's Hockey Association	10,954
Hockey Association	5,081
All England Netball Association	850 (15 May 1954)

It at once becomes clear that there is a very big range of wealth among governing bodies and this is reflected in what they spend, for instance, on coaching. In 1958–9 the Football Association spent £12,290 in this way and the Lawn Tennis Association £5,834. It is also clear that the rich bodies are those whose sports command a gate. Other sports which may be no less satisfying and no less worthy are poor either because they do not attract spectators (hockey) or because large numbers of spectators cannot be accommodated (basketball), or because the pockets of the spectators cannot be reached (rowing). The Oxford and Cambridge Boat Race which has annually for more than a hundred years attracted vast crowds of spectators, more than most other great sporting events, has brought little or no money to the two Boat Clubs or to the Amateur Rowing Association. No gates can be charged on the tow-path of the Thames and the riparian property owners have pocketed their own takings. As the costs of administration and of coaching and recruiting new performers rise the logical conclusion of *laissez-faire* is to make participation dependent upon the ability to entertain. Such a development would, of course, change the very nature of sport and alter its personal and social functions.

British participation in international events other than

Olympic Games and Commonwealth Games is financed by the governing body concerned. Here again adequate representation depends upon gate money. In 1958–9 the Lawn Tennis Association received £49,576 (subject to tax) from the 1958 Wimbledon Championships. The Football Association received £509,244 from international challenge cup and other matches and the Rugby Union had a surplus of about £60,000 from its international matches at Twickenham.

Representation in the Olympic Games and the Commonwealth Games is organized by the British Olympic Association and financed by appeals for voluntary subscriptions. The cost of sending a British entrant to the Olympic Games in Los Angeles in 1932 was £85, to Melbourne in 1956 it was £624. A similar estimate for sending a competitor to the Commonwealth Games in Australia in 1962 was £400.

To send an entrant to international games is one task, to win a medal is another and more expensive. In retrospect it is possible to estimate how much some medals have cost. Swimming provides a good example. After World War II British swimmers were unable to give their competitors a reasonable contest in international events. Three men, including Britain's Olympic Coach in 1948, consulted together to improve British swimming and gain an Olympic gold medal within ten years. The Amateur Swimming Association approved their scheme of group training. The best swimmers and their coaches were invited to train together as a residential centre for a single spell of fourteen days. These courses were repeated, the standard of swimming rose. In ten years £6,000 of voluntary funds were used and in 1956 Judy Grinham brought back from Melbourne a gold medal which she won in the hundred-metre back-stroke race. The Australians, however, had launched a more lavish project known as the Townsville Scheme by which potential Olympic swimmers were brought together and trained intensively in the best conditions for six months before the great contest. Thirty swimmers were so trained in 1956 at a cost of £200 per head. The Townsville Scheme thus spent £6,000 of voluntary funds in six months. The Australian swimmers won eight gold medals.* It is not possible to tell in advance the exact sum necessary to ensure success in competitive sport. It is clear enough, however, that gold medals have a price and that so long as expenditure on training is unregulated by protocol or convention the price will rise in proportion to the amount of money that the controlling bodies or the central governments of the countries are prepared to set aside for them. No financial profit now comes to sporting bodies from the Olympic Games themselves. The last festival to make a profit was that held in London in 1948 when a modest £29,000 profit was shared among the sporting bodies after the government had deducted income tax. Subsequent Olympic Games have all been run at a financial loss.

In the main, the day-to-day expenses of sport in Britain are met by those who take part in it or who watch it. Many facilities, however, especially school gymnasia and swimming-baths, are provided by local authorities from the rates and indirectly also from taxes. The central government makes grants to local education authorities in part payment of certain expenditure. Government expenditure during 1959–60 on facilities for recreative, social and physical training was in £000s—

COUNTIES	COUNTY BOROUGH	LONDON	TOTAL
£2,552	£2,587	£1,164	£6,303,000

This expenditure embraced facilities for activities other than sport but most of the money was devoted to sport. Local authorities also received loan sanctions amounting to some

*
100-m free style	J. Henricks	4×200-m relay	National team
400-m free style	M. Rose	100-m free style (women)	D. Fraser
1,500-m free style	M. Rose	400-m free-style (women)	L. Crapp
100-m back stroke	D. Thiele	4×100-m relay (women)	National team

£4½ million to provide swimming-baths and facilities for physical training and recreation. In addition the Ministry of Education made certain grants under the Physical Training and Recreation Act as follows—

Playing Fields and other sports facilities . .	70,569
Coaching Schemes in athletics, fencing, lawn tennis, swimming, judo, horse riding and table tennis .	13,100
Grants to the headquarters of national bodies—	
Central Council of Physical Recreation . .	140,000
Others	21,000
Grants to voluntary youth organizations . .	176,525

No public funds whatever were available for assisting British representation at international events. Government financial assistance is seen to be based on the educational system of the country and to be very limited in amount and in scope. To see government expenditure in perspective two further points should be kept in mind. The first is that the government collects more than £30 million annually from taxes on sport, including betting taxes. Until 1960 a fundamental principle of fiscal policy had been to have general revenue and not to allocate specific revenues to specific expenditure. In 1960, however, the government laid a special levy on bookmakers expected to bring in £1,250,000 in order to help the industry or the sport of horse-racing to survive. This measure has served to underline the haphazard assistance of the state to sport.

The second point of view is outward-looking. In all but three Western European countries the football pools are controlled by the state, which allocates a proportion of the profits to sport. In Sweden, for instance, this sum amounted to about £855,000 in 1959–60 and in Norway to about £468,000 in 1961. The three exceptions are France, Portugal and Great Britain. Inhibitions about the state helping to finance international representation or any other manifestation of sport are rarely found in countries other than Britain, least of all in the communist countries. *Pravda* stated in July, 1954: "The Communist Party and the Soviet Government regard sports as one of the important means of communist education. The allocation for health measures and physical culture in this year's budget surpasses 29,000 million roubles" (about £2,590 million).

External comparisons and internal pressures induced both major political parties in Britain to suggest an annual government grant of £5 million to sport. The suggestions were made before the general election of 1958 and little was heard of them afterwards. Similar pressures induced the Wolfenden Committee on Sport to recommend that £5 million should be distributed to sport from exchequer funds. The novel feature of the Wolfenden Committee's Report was the recommendation that a Sports Development Council should be established to allocate grants of money. Dissatisfaction with the previous record of Government Ministries and the Ministry of Education in particular, the narrowness of their terms of reference, the haphazard nature and the inadequate amount of their subventions led the Committee to favour entirely new machinery for aiding sport.

In summary the increasing affluence of society is reflected in the proliferation of sports and the larger number of people participating in them. Men and women, boys and girls can and do spend far more money on sport than they used to. Nevertheless, the increased cost of facilities in a concentrated and urbanized country and the impossibility of the immediate participants in any one sport finding and organizing sufficient resources to meet the cost of facilities means that even an affluent society must make general provision for sport if all its members are to have the opportunity of enjoying it, and if the best performers are to meet the challenge of world standards.

There must be a postscript to this examination of sport and

affluence. The findings are immediately relevant to perhaps ten per cent of the world's population. In 1957 only ten countries, topped by the United States, enjoyed a gross national product of more than $1,000 *per capita*. Most people live in countries where the gross national product is less than $100 *per capita*. The figure for the U.S.A. in 1957 was $2,343, for India $72, for China $56 and for Burma $52.

Organized sport costs money and is, therefore, in spite of an enormous and world-wide expansion, still out of reach of most men and women. Many of the poor, if they have food and energy, play some form of organized game modified to suit their own environment, but many more, if they enjoy sport at all, do so in a spontaneous, unorganized and unrefined form.

BIBLIOGRAPHY

1. MOLYNEUX, D. D., The Development of Physical Recreation in the Birmingham District 1871–92, unpublished thesis, University of Birmingham p. 84.

2. ANDERSON, N., *Work and Leisure*, pp. 250–1 (London, 1961).

3. ABRAMS, M., *The Teenage Consumer* (London, 1959).

4. HER MAJESTY'S STATIONERY OFFICE, *Education in* 1960 (London, 1961).

See also

HER MAJESTY'S STATIONERY OFFICE, *Annual Reports of Ministry of Education* (London).

PHYSICAL EDUCATION ASSOCIATION OF GREAT BRITAIN AND NORTHERN IRELAND, *Britain in the World of Sport* (London, 1956).

Journals of American Association for Health, Physical Education and Recreation, Washington, D.C. (Issues for 1962).

POLITICAL AND ECONOMIC PLANNING, *The Cricket Industry* Vol. XXII, No. 401 (August, 1956).

POLITICAL AND ECONOMIC PLANNING, *The Football Industry* Vol. XVII, No. 324 (February, 1951).

WOLFENDEN COMMITTEE, *Sport and the Community* (London, 1960).

XII

FITNESS AND SPORT

THE postscript to the previous chapter indicated the startling gap between the most and the least affluent countries. The gap in basic physical fitness of the normally healthy population in the two categories of country is becoming almost as startling. An American sent out to Africa to give "technical assistance" reported on his return in March, 1962—

> My assignment was to bring "technical assistance" to some of the peoples of Africa. I found that they needed this assistance but I found there was a great lesson to be learned from them about the thing we call fitness.
>
> In Tanganyika boys and girls play field hockey in mixed teams; they do not use free substitution and girls ask no quarter. Boys fifteen years old compete in the ten-thousand-metres race. And why not when they have to walk or run ten miles a day to school each day?
>
> In Ethiopia, when Adebe Bikila, Olympic Marathon champion went for a work-out, he was followed by a horde of young boys who were still at his heels forty-five minutes later . . .
>
> The people I worked with in Africa . . . in many cases were, by our standards, under educated, underfed, under clothed and under nourished. But they can travel fifty miles a day on foot; they can survive extreme weather conditions; they can run a deer to exhaustion . . . They are, quite simply, fit.[1]

The writer implied that in physical fitness the term under-developed would be more correctly applied to the United States than to Ethiopia. This was a subjective impression. Judged by another criterion, success in the Olympic Games, competitors from the underdeveloped countries with a subsistence economy have not done as well as those from industrial or agricultural countries. Nevertheless, a survey of results in the Olympic Games in Helsinki of 1952 showed that the difference in point level, that is the average number of points per participation, between the rich and the poor was not so large as had been expected. Had it been possible for the countries on a subsistence economy to tap the full potential of fit citizens for training and representation in the Olympic Games the difference might have been removed or even reversed. The United States government and people have certainly become particularly self-conscious about the physical state of American citizens and many tests have been carried out which indicate that for all the money spent on sport and recreation the American is not fit and is becoming less fit. Deprivation and necessity train heart and muscle: indulgence and affluence do not.

In December, 1953 and May, 1954 two articles appeared in American Physical Education Journals outlining the Kraus–Weber Tests of Minimum Muscular Fitness.[2 & 3] The researches of Dr. Kraus and Dr. Weber extended beyond the United States to children in Austria, and Italy. They purported to show that 56.6 per cent of American children failed one or more of these tests, while only 8 per cent of the European children failed; 16.4 per cent of the American youngsters failed two or more tests.

The results of the Kraus–Weber Tests aroused great interest and concern in the United States but the tests and the interpretation of their results were not above suspicion. The American Association of Health, Physical Education and Recreation, therefore, devised their own battery of tests to be administered to a nation-wide sample of boys and girls between the ages of ten and seventeen. These tended to confirm the low level of fitness of U.S. children in so far as it could be tested in this way. The same tests were made on over ten thousand British boys and girls in 1958. Standardization of testing in such a large project was difficult and the precise figures for the comparative performance of British and

American boys and girls were quite unreliable, but the general conclusion that British boys and girls were superior to U.S. boys in all tests except the soft ball throw and had greater shoulder strength, agility, abdominal endurance, leg power and circulatory endurance may have been true. In Denmark the same tests were administered to three hundred and nineteen boys and one hundred and thirty-four girls by Howard Knuttgen who found that seventy per cent of boys' scores and eighty-six per cent of girls' scores exceeded the various American mean scores. Nevertheless, the fact that performers in later tests may have been motivated by the knowledge that they were to be compared with the earlier American performers made any true comparison impossible and it was the absolute not the comparative standards of performance which gave cause for alarm.

Physical softness is not a problem that plagued children alone in America. The Metropolitan Life Insurance Company estimated that a fourth of Americans were too fat and that one of every two adults was overweight. A research worker at the Veterans' Administration Center, Martinsburg, estimated that fifteen million persons in the United States were obese, i.e. ten per cent or more over the average weight for those of the same age and sex and height, while another five million were more than twenty per cent overweight.

Perhaps the most devastating statistics came from a report of a Congressional hearing concerned with selective service. It was revealed that the United States needed to call up seven men to obtain two soldiers and that of the five who were rejected three were turned down for physical reasons and two for mental disabilities. The rejection rate was more than double that of World War II and was increasing year by year. Congressmen were told that in order to recruit 196,000 additional men to meet the Berlin crisis which arose in 1959 the government had to call up 755,000.

The Americans have been more assiduous than any other nation in devising tests and applying them to their citizens. The lack of fitness of citizens of the United States is thus exposed for all to see. There is no reason to think, however, that other affluent societies in Britain or Western Europe are escaping the insidious flabbiness which has begun to characterize the United States.

There is no great mystery about the causes of the physical decline of the West. The decrease of casual exercise coupled with indulgence in food and drink more than offsets any physical toughening which may result from increased participation in sport. One hundred years ago everyone everywhere walked to work. Most people in the world still do. The modern city-dweller, however, does not.

Often he does not walk at all if he can avoid it. "We are faced with a curious paradox," writes Lewis Mumford, "the new suburban form has now produced an anti-urban pattern. With the destruction of walking distances has gone the destruction of walking as a normal means of circulation: the motor-car has made it unsafe and the extension of the suburb has made it impossible."[4] At places of work lifting and handling are reduced to a minimum by the service of machines; facilities for refreshment and often for recreation exist on the site and architecture at home and at work eliminates climbing.

Modern architecture is horizontal. Buildings may be tall to look at, but within them vertical movement is only possible because it is mechanized. If the present trend continues, climbing more than one flight of stairs will cease. The Harvard step test involving stepping up on to a bench twenty inches high and down again at one-second intervals is commonly taken to be a good measure of fitness and it is certainly one of the commonest of fitness tests. If this assumption is correct, then the elimination of stair-climbing from daily life must be an important factor in the softening process.

Economic factors and social pressures have accelerated the trend towards horizontal architecture, but the trend has been helped by the bad image attached to stair-climbing. The activity is associated with mothers struggling up and down with children or shopping baskets, with the incapacity of the old, with the rush up and down at the beginning and end of school, with the approach to office imprisonment and with hurrying to catch trams. At one English boarding school on a hill there was a boys' rule that everyone must go up the steps to library and chapel four steps at a time. The school produced a succession of good hurdlers. Stair-climbing, however, is not generally regarded as good training for anything and is to be avoided even more than is walking the streets.

Transport is the second factor which has reduced casual exercise. The use of public transport has increased throughout the century but the production and use of private transport have been comparatively recent and have increased at a high rate. Between 1948 and 1958 American car ownership increased from thirty million to sixty-seven million and at a holiday period most of the cars were on the road.[5]

The appeal of the motor-car is not so much to man's indolence as to his appetite for self-expression. Professor L. P. Jacks said: "Man is a skill hungry animal." Fifty years ago it was almost impossible to satisfy this hunger without taking exercise, and usually a deal of exercise. Even train and tramcar drivers stood up while they drove their vehicles, and horses exercised the coachman or cabbie even while he sat down. The invention of the internal combustion engine changed all that. Motor-cycle, scooter and car now provide opportunities for the exercise of skill without extending the cardiovascular system more than sitting at a table extends it. Hardly any local strength or endurance is required but the driver satisfies his hunger for skilled activity and for self-expression. Often, too often for the safety of road users, the motor-cyclist or car-driver exercises his skill in a competitive spirit as though he were taking part in a sport. But transport has none of the redeeming features of sport, neither the rules nor the defined area of unreality. The rules of the road are made for a non-sporting purpose and are, therefore, broken by the competitive driver in a way that could not be tolerated in a genuine sport.

The world of sport itself now contains an increasing number of mechanized and semi-mechanized sports such as water-ski-ing, aqua-lung diving, go-kart racing. Other sports like ski-ing and golf have their mechanical aids which reduce their exercise potential for many performers. The sports which have increased their following vastly in the seventeen years after World War II as shown in Chapter XI have been some of the least strenuous. Boats, other than the smaller and less stable din-ghies, canoes and racing rowing-boats, provide little exercise, angling is a gentle sport, ten-pin bowling is not vigorous and golf on many courses in the United States has been deprived of its energetic side by the provision of mechanical transport for golfers. Even in sport the tendency has been to eliminate the action of putting one foot in front of the other as a form of locomotion.

Television has frequently been blamed for causing an increase in watching and a decrease in doing various activities. Almost certainly it has reduced the amount of casual exercise that people take but not by a very great amount. Hilde Himmelweit in her classic investigation into the effect of television on children found in comparing "viewers" with "controls" that unorganized activities such as walking or being out with friends were reduced in the lives of the "viewers." Sport was much less affected and competitive sport held its own with younger children and suffered a barely significant setback with adolescents. Indeed, television appeared to stimulate an interest in sport. When swimming and skating were examined—and they were selected because of their frequency on television—both "viewers" and "controls" preferred doing to watching in similar proportions. About seventy per cent of all groups throughout the intelligence range of those questioned preferred to take part rather than to be spectators.[6] Among adults the probability is that television makes more serious inroads into casual exercise but it is very doubtful whether it has any negative effect upon participation in sport.

Apologists for sport often plead its contribution to health, or fitness. All the three terms, sport, health and fitness are imprecise and a careful examination of the claim shows that in many respects it is hard to substantiate. The physical vigour and fitness of those inhabitants of the so-called "under-developed" countries noted at the beginning of the chapter is coupled with an expectation of life much less than that in countries where physical softness is setting in (*see* Table IV). As far as national averages are concerned longevity and softness appear to go together. In Holland, Sweden, New

TABLE IV

Length of Life of Men and Women in Selected Countries[10]

Country	Year	Individual Average (Male)	Individual Average (Female)
Netherlands	1953–5	71·0	73·9
Sweden	1951–5	70·5	73·4
New Zealand	1950–2	68·3	72·4
England and Wales	1956	67·8	73·3
Canada	1955	67·6	73·0
United States	1954–5	66·7	72·9
Australia	1946–8	66·1	70·6
Thailand	1947–8	48·7	51·9
Guatemala	1949–51	43·8	43·5
Congo	1950–2	37·6	40·0
India	1941–50	32·5	31·7

Zealand, England, Canada and the United States and Australia, a man's expectation of life is more than sixty-five. In the Congo and India it is less than forty.

In many countries the expectation of life is improving. In the United States, for instance, there has been a mortality decline of forty-six per cent in fifty years. It would be difficult to maintain that participation in sport has markedly affected this trend. Investigations into the mortality of athletes and non-athletes when it shows a difference between the longevity of the two categories does not settle the problem because an athlete may be a different kind of person genetically and this difference may have something to do with his becoming an athlete in the first place.

One of the commonest forms of disorder in later life is cardiovascular breakdown. J. N. Morris of the Social Medicine Research Unit analysed the records of illness of 31,000 bus drivers and conductors in the London Transport Service during 1949. The drivers had a higher rate of coronary heart disease (2.7 per 1,000) than conductors (1.9 per 1,000) and Morris adopted the hypothesis that men employed in relatively sedentary occupations had more coronary heart disease than men who held jobs requiring a moderate amount of physical activity. This was a statement of association not of cause and effect. Morris and his associates did not mention the possibility that physical activity might protect against coronary heart disease.[7] Later on they reported that drivers and conductors differed in at least one other respect. It was found that the trouser waist size of uniforms of drivers was larger than that of conductors at all ages. Drivers might, therefore, bring to their job characteristics which predisposed them to a higher rate of coronary heart disease.[8] Other research has failed to establish a cause-and-effect relationship between physical activity and the reduction of coronary heart disease and suggests that if it is established the beneficial effects of exercise must be small when compared to the dimensions of the problem. Nevertheless, it is recognized that emotional stress is an important factor in coronary disease and there are good theoretic grounds for believing that the increase of vagus tone produced by physical training may help to protect the heart against the effects of stress. Furthermore, if sport and physical recreation contribute to personal serenity and a satisfying philosophy of life, they can certainly reduce stress. At the same time it could be true that training in the techniques of relaxation might have a more beneficial effect upon the incidence of heart disease than training for sport. One proposition in favour of sport does, however, seem to have now been established: exercise and hard training do not bring on heart disease.

Prevention or control of obesity is another effect which is hoped for from exercise and sport. There is no doubt that exercise consumes calories. Examples of energy expenditure over the basal metabolic rate are dressing and undressing 30–40 Calories per hour, washing up 60 Calories per hour, walking 270 Calories, swimming (crawl) 700–900 Calories, squash rackets 600–700 Calories, rowing at peak effort 1,200 Calories. Calories are consumed whenever exercise is taken and half an hour of squash per day would consume sixteen pounds of fat in a year. Moreover, the heavier a man is the more energy will be required to move weight and his total energy expenditure will be greater than that of a lightly built man. The loss of weight, therefore, depends upon whether intake of food is increased or not when exercise is increased. Such an increase certainly happens but not automatically and there is a range within which intake does not increase in proportion to output. Activity will then reduce body weight. What is more significant is that cessation of activity and the adoption of a sedentary life is not accompanied beyond a certain point by a reduction of intake. The obesity of an

ex-Rugby footballer who has gone to seed is not attributable
to the game he once played but to his failure to reduce his
liquid and solid intake when he put his boots away for the

TABLE V

Calorie Requirements for Various Activities[10]

Calorie values to be added to B.M.R. + 10 per cent for S.D.A.

Occupation	Cal. per hr.	Occupation	Cal. per hr.
Domestic		*Sports*	
Sewing	10–30	Walking, 4 m.p.h.	350
Writing	20	Running	800–1,000
Sitting at rest	15	Cycling—	
Standing relaxed	20	10 m.p.h.	450
Dressing and undressing	30–40	14 m.p.h.	700
Ironing (5-lb iron)	60	Horse-riding	
Dish washing	60	Walk	150
Sweeping or dusting	80–130	Trot	500
Polishing	150–200	Gallop	600
		Dancing	200–400
Industrial		Gymnastics	200–500
Tailoring	50–100	Golf	300
Shoe-making	80–100	Tennis	400–500
Book-binding	75–100	Soccer	550
Locksmith	150–200	Canoeing	
House painter	150–200	2.5 m.p.h.	180
Carpenter	200	4 m.p.h.	420
Joiner	200	Rowing (peak effort)	1200
Cartwright	250–300	Swimming	
Smith (heavy work)	300–400	Breast or back	300–650
Riveting	300	Crawl	700–900
Coal mining	200–400	Squash rackets	600–700
Stone mason	300–400	Climbing	700–900
Sawing wood	400–600	Ski-ing	600–700
		Skating (fast)	600–700
		Wrestling	900–1,000

last time. Dr. Jean Mayer, Professor of Nutrition at Harvard
University, has been "convinced that inactivity is the most
important factor explaining the frequency of creeping over-

weight in modern Western societies." He has pointed out that the regulation of food intake was not evolved to adapt to the mechanized and sedentary life of today and continues—

> Adaptions to these conditions without development of obesity means that either the individual will have to step up his activity or that he will be mildly or acutely hungry all his life . . . if the first alternative is difficult it is well to remember that the second alternative is so much more difficult that to rely on it for weight control programs can only continue to lead to the fiascos of the past.[9]

For a more detailed and more extensive treatment of the relationship of sport to fitness the reader is referred to the symposium on *Exercise and Fitness* published by the University of Illinois in 1960. The relationship is still imperfectly understood even by those who are researching in the field. The problem is not made easier by the fact that *fit* and *fitness* are English concepts and English words which defy easy translation into other languages and have a number of different meanings even for those whose native tongue is English.

Nevertheless, there is widespread concern about the debilitating effect of modern industrial civilization. Witnesses to this concern are the commercial health clubs and clinics, the programmes of voluntary clubs and organizations for physical recreation and the action of governments, notably those of the U.S.A. and U.S.S.R., in promoting sports and fitness programmes. On 3rd March, 1961, President John F. Kennedy named Charles B. Wilkinson as his special consultant on physical fitness and initiated a nation-wide physical fitness programme. The U.S.S.R. initiated its own fitness programme with a system of G.T.O. awards for games and sports— "Ready for Labour and Defence"—in 1930-1. In Britain, apart from the setting up of a National Fitness Council in 1937 which disappeared two years later, initiative has been left to voluntary organizations and local authorities. National fitness has not so far (1962) been regarded as a matter of urgency. Whether sport by itself can counteract the softening effect of modern life to the extent that individuals and governments want counteraction is doubtful. It is more likely that either specific therapeutic exercise, not sport, will be needed or the community and its members will have to be content with a much lower level of fitness than they have been accustomed to in the past. If the second alternative comes about the pattern of sport may change radically so that the less physically demanding sports are practised by more people at an earlier age than at present in the more highly developed societies, while the less highly developed societies adopt and excel at the sports which the West can no longer sustain.

BIBLIOGRAPHY

1. *Journal of American Association for Health, Physical Education and Recreation* **33**, 3, p. 20 (March 1962).
2. *Journal of American Association for Health, Physical Education and Recreation* (December 1953).
3. AMERICAN ASSOCIATION FOR HEALTH, PHYSICAL EDUCATION AND RECREATION, *Research Quarterly* (May, 1954).
4. MUMFORD, LEWIS, *The City in History*, p. 506 (London, 1961).
5. OWEN, W., Automotive Transport in the United States, *Annals of American Academy of Political and Social Science*. **320**, pp. 1–8 (November 1958).
6. HIMMELWEIT, H., OPPENHEIM, A. N. and VINCE P., *Television and the Child*, p. 346 (Oxford, 1958).
7. MORRIS, J. N. *et al.*, Coronary Heart Disease and Physical Activity of Work, *Lancet*, **2** (1953).
8. MORRIS, J. N. *et. al.*, Physique of London Busmen: Epidemiology of Uniforms, *Lancet*, **2** (1956).
9. MAYER, J., Exercise and Weight Control, in *Exercise and Fitness* pp. 120–1 (University of Illinois, 1960).
10. UNIVERSITY OF ILLINOIS, *Exercise and Fitness*, p. 54 (1960).
See also
   JOHNSON, W., *Science and Medicine of Exercise and Sports* (New York, 1960).

XIII

URBAN LIFE AND LEISURE

In the year 1800 no city in the Western world had more than a million inhabitants. London, the largest city, had 959,310 inhabitants. By 1850 London had two million and Paris one million. Fifty years later the number of metropolises with more than one million inhabitants had risen to eleven and to twenty-seven in 1930. By 1950 in the United States 83,929,863 people lived in 168 urban areas with 50,000 inhabitants or more. In the world at large 13.1 per cent of the whole population lived in cities of more than one million inhabitants. The comparable figure for 1800 was 1.7 per cent. In England and Wales in 1959 no more than nine million people out of a total forty-five million inhabitants lived in truly rural areas. More than sixteen million people lived in conurbations.

Greater London now occupies about six hundred and thirteen square miles and unless preventive measures of town planning are taken a large stretch of England from London in the south-east to Manchester in the north-west will become one great conurbation. New York and its suburbs now cover about 2,514 square miles and the whole eastern coastal strip from Maine to Florida could become a single conurbation.

At the same time as men have drifted towards the towns they have paradoxically set store by low-density building for living in the belief that it offers a richer life. One result is to be seen in Los Angeles where a density of five houses to the acre has been widely adopted and private cars have supplanted public transport. More than one-third of Los Angeles is consumed by transportation facilities and two-thirds of the central area is occupied by streets, free ways, parking facilities and garages. Furthermore, an increasing amount of land is wanted for offices, warehouses, shops and factories. Inevitably social and recreative facilities are scattered and existing recreative facilities may be usurped for other purposes.

The problem of providing adequate outdoor facilities for games and sports has become insuperable in some urban areas. For London the problem can be stated simply. The National Playing Fields Association recommended a standard of six acres of playing space and one acre of park and public garden for every thousand of the population. In 1945 London accepted this standard of seven acres per thousand and decided that four of these acres might be provided within the County of London and the other three should be provided outside. By 1960 the London County Council had provided somewhat more than two and a half acres of open space per thousand of the population, but sixteen of the twenty-eight boroughs within London had far less than the standard. Islington, worse provided than any other borough, had no more than three-tenths acres per thousand of its citizens. To bring all boroughs up to standard the Council would have had to create another two and a quarter thousand acres of open space. A second aim was to provide three-quarters of an acre of playing field for every hundred school children in secondary schools. To achieve this aim more than three thousand additional acres of playing fields were needed. Both aims become more impossible to achieve as each year the appetite of roads, car parks and other space-eaters increases. Taking into account that grass pitches can be played on for no more than about ten hours a week if they are to remain playable from year to year it is indisputable that for London and other great conurbations the playing of field games can cater only for a very limited number of the population. Some games normally played on grass can be played on hard porous pitches or on tarmacadam surfaces and the replacement of grass by such surfaces allows more intensive use of the land available. If the areas are floodlit they can be used still more intensively. Nevertheless, if the inhabitants of conurbations are to play games and take part in sport to any great extent within those conurbations then the great need is for indoor facilities. These can be built one above the other as towers of flats or offices are built. They may also form a part of an office or dwelling block without occupying any additional land.

A tall block of flats is a vertical street with a tramway up the centre and no gardens or backyards. Even the old style horizontal streets which in many towns and villages were a children's playground as well as a highway have become unsafe and unsuitable for play. In many areas town planning authorities now make it obligatory for developers of industrial blocks to provide space for parking cars within or around the buildings. In one or two areas a similar requirement has been made for the provision of facilities for sport and recreation which the cars have made so necessary if the level of physical fitness to which we have been accustomed is to be maintained.

Local authorities, large and small, have themselves taken the initiative in providing indoor facilities "round the corner." In Britain the commonest procedure is for the local authority to provide multi-purpose gymnasia in new schools and to make them available in the evening and on Saturdays for those who are no longer at school. Elsewhere, local authorities have established multi-sports centres which are independent of schools but which can be used by them. The city council of West Berlin, for instance, has built multi-sports halls in each of its twelve administrative districts and is building smaller gymnastic halls on existing playing fields to be available for different sections of the population from nine in the morning until ten at night with some hours' use on Saturdays and Sundays.

In towns and cities where the climate is more equable than it is in northern Europe or much of north America indoor facilities may not be so urgently needed, but wherever land hunger becomes acute central and local governments are taking the initiative and sometimes providing the necessary money to ensure that facilities for sport are available near the dwellings of their citizens. There is little evidence that the demand for facilities has anywhere been saturated.[1]

If the nature of towns and cities has changed in the last hundred years so have work and leisure. In 1850 men in the United States worked a little less than seventy hours a week. Most workers, therefore, worked from six a.m. to six p.m. for six days in the week. Some worked for ten hours on all seven days. In 1950 the estimated average number of hours worked in a week was forty, which was the equivalent of five eight-hour days. The figure takes no account of the difference between agricultural and non-agricultural workers. The average for non-agricultural workers was 38.8 hours per week.[2] It was not entirely fanciful for the President of the British Medical Association to forecast in 1962 that in a short time a man would be working a twenty-hour week in the United States and a two-hour day in Russia.[3] A similar ratio of work to leisure was achieved for a large number of citizens in the imperial city of Rome during the second and third centuries A. D. It will not be long before machines are exploited as efficiently as human slaves were in the past.

Not merely has there been an increase in the amount of leisure, but the relationship of work to leisure has changed. The factory workers may never have had an intense interest in their work but because of its nature and their long hours at it they were absorbed and dominated by it. They have now come to terms with their work in the sense that they can more easily abandon all thought of it when they leave their factory or workshop. The modern workers have more potential mental and physical energy for their leisure. They, therefore, provide a large force which may be and, to some extent is being, recruited to pursuits including games and sports which were previously beyond their emotional and physical resources.

J. K. Galbraith in *The Affluent Society* has suggested that as leisure has increased a new class has emerged. Nearly all societies at all times have had a leisured class exempt from work but such exemption is no longer desired or respectable. The new class consists of men and women whose work is not painful, fatiguing or accompanied by mental or physical discomfort. On the contrary it is for the most part interesting and carries with it social status. In the nineteenth century in England and the United States the class consisted of a handful of educators, clerics, writers and artists. In 1960 the number of those whose primary identification is with work of this nature is undoubtedly in the millions. The growth of this class has greatly increased the catchments for games and sports which were devised for and by the middle classes of earlier generations.

Another factor of importance for sport is the distribution of leisure. The number of hours in the working day has been somewhat reduced leaving more time and energy available for leisure pursuits in the evenings. More significant has been the increase in the number of whole days on which no work is done. Holidays with pay and long week-ends have enabled men and women to adopt pursuits and sports which cannot be enjoyed in an evening or even on a half-day's holiday. It is this pattern of leisure which has made possible in Europe and America the great growth of sports and pastimes which take place far from city streets and office blocks. The Athletic Association of Chicago estimated the following figures for the number of participants in selected sports in the United States—

	1946	1956	1959
Boating	20,000,000	28,000,000	37,000,000
Fishing	13,100,000	20,813,000	25,620,000
Hunting	9,990,000	11,784,000	18,000,000
Ski-ing	1,400,000	2,180,000	3,000,000
Golf	4,300,000	5,100,000	—

Boating includes many activities which are not strictly sport. Driving a motor-boat is no more akin to sport than driving a car round the countryside. There is no doubt, however, that true sports using boats have increased considerably. Golf has been associated with towns and cities but the time taken to play a round is such that the game is precluded for those whose leisure is short and the game has drawn many recruits as a result of the new pattern of leisure. The increase in the number of golfers, however, is not so spectacular as increases in the other sports listed.

In the summer of 1960 about ninety per cent of all Americans participated in some form of outdoor recreation. The Outdoor Recreation Review Commission whose report was presented to Congress in 1962 estimated that these Americans participated in one outdoor activity or another on 4.4 billion separate occasions.

Britain has experienced a similar boom in sports which can be followed only at week-ends or on holidays. Mountaineering, potholing, sailing, ski-ing, canoeing and gliding have drawn an increasing number of adherents each year. Scotland in particular has begun to realize its potential as a holiday sports centre. Ski-lifts and access roads have been constructed on mountain slopes which before the war had few visitors save ptarmigans, mountain hares and snow buntings. In six years from 1955 to 1961 the number of people using camps and hostels in National Forest Parks in Scotland rose from 85,500 to more than a quarter of a million.

The Central Council of Physical Recreation began to cater for holiday sport immediately after the war and organized in 1946 an experimental sports training holiday in the Isle of Wight. The demand for such holidays grew steadily each year and now forms an important part of the Council's total programme. Other holiday organizations have taken up the idea. Some but not all of the training offered in these holidays is for the traditional team games, racket games and combat sports, not for outdoor activities and "conquest" sports.

The boom in camping, fishing, sailing, mountaineering and ski-ing in places as far apart as the Appalachian Mountains in America, the Cairngorms in Scotland and the Bavarian Alps is only partly accounted for by holidays with pay. The cult of the week-end has also made its contribution. In late Victorian days and in the Edwardian age the week-end was the prerogative of English aristocracy. The *Oxford Dictionary* gives 1878 for the first use of the term. In the 1920s the forty-hour week and the motor-car in America put the countryside within reach of townsmen for two days out of seven a generation before people elsewhere could exploit the week-end. Since that time one country after another has developed a week-end pattern of behaviour. In Italy *il week-end* has not yet been fully accepted but full employment and prosperity are still novel and do not affect the whole country. In France the school children's traditional holiday on a Thursday has hampered the development of the week-end but French campers have increased from one million to about three million in ten years. A substantial number of these camp at week-ends. The Germans, certainly those within easy rail travel of mountains, have gone ski-ing on Sundays in great numbers since the 1930s and the week-end has extended a pattern of vigorous and sporting behaviour which was already well developed. An important characteristic of the week-end is that it is often a family occasion. Sports or club premises for sport which can cater for adults with children of different physical abilities and strengths have already met a social need and are likely to be in greater demand. The sailing club with its junior classes, the ski-ing centre which caters for children, the mountain hostels where both children's expeditions and adult climbs can be undertaken provide the kind of facility for week-end sport which is likely to be needed in the future.

The exodus of so many citizens from the towns at week-ends has not, in Britain, resulted in a diminution of week-end games of cricket and football. Such games may not have grown in number recently. Limitation of space and pitches rather than lack of interest has been the handicap. Week-end games of football in London Parks during the winter of 1956–7 amounted to twenty-two thousand, and week-end games of cricket amounted to eight-thousand. Tennis courts within the urban areas and golf courses on their fringes have been fully used on Saturdays and Sundays. The enthusiasm for football, most of which must inevitably be played at week-ends, is particularly strong among boys who leave school at fifteen or sixteen. The Crowther Committee found that thirty-one per cent of one sample of young men had continued to play team games for at least three years after leaving school, a considerably higher percentage than the figure for active membership of youth organizations in general. It is clear, then, that since the end of World War II the out-of-town sports have supplemented but not supplanted the Saturday and Sunday games which have been played during the last eighty or one hundred years.

Even in the 1960s most townsmen have leisure on five days in the week in the evenings only. In Britain and in many other regions, for six or seven months in the year the evenings are dark and the weather inclement. In London increasing demand for organized leisure activities under professional leadership or instruction is reflected in the number of hours' instruction given in evening institutes. The total number of hours almost doubled between 1947–8 and 1960–1, and in the latter year amounted to more than three–quarters of a million. The activities, ranging from accountancy to zoology, numbered six hundred and thirty-two and include classes in forty different forms of sport, gymnastics and dance. These physical activites accounted for about forty per cent of all enrolments for all classes. The sports involved were those which could be pursued indoors or on hard surfaces under floodlights. Within these limitations evening sport shared in the general increase of organized leisure.

The present pattern in Britain as elsewhere has been partly determined by what facilities and leadership have been available. Basket-ball might be more frequently played in Britain if more halls were available where it could be played. On the other hand the very great increase in the popularity of judo and weight-lifting throughout Europe is not to be accounted for by the availability of facilities. Boxing and wrestling might have been accommodated within many of the same premises. There are fashions in sport as well as in clothes. There are local traditions, too, and these may give momentum to one sport in one town and to another in a neighbouring district. The difficulties in the way of generalizing about evening sport are considerable but the pattern of instructional classes in London's evening institutes gives an indication of what sports people do in one large urban area of three and a quarter million inhabitants. Table VI shows that the nine most popular activities were dancing, recreative gymnastics for men, table tennis, football training either indoors or on playgrounds under floodlights, badminton, gymnastics and "keep-fit" activities for women, judo, boxing, weight-

M

lifting and fencing. All these activities had more than one
hundred classes each. None of the other forty activities for

TABLE VI

Physical Recreation Classes in London's Evening Institutes

Activities commanding more than 100 different classes in winter 1960

Activity	Number of Classes Organized		
Dancing—			
Ballroom		267	
English folk	6		
Old time	113		
National	83		
Square	4		
Other dancing for men and women	94		
	—	300	
Other dancing for women only		94	661
Recreative gymnastics for men			364
Table tennis			358
Football training			341
Badminton			312
Recreative gymnastics and keep-fit classes for women			250
Judo			228
Boxing			182
Weight-lifting			144
Total number of classes organized in all physical activities			3,278

The activities are, in the main, those which can be pursued in school
gymnasia and playgrounds, some of which are floodlit.

which instructional classes were organized reached the
century. Swimming, which was very popular, does not appear
in the list because it took place almost entirely in swimming-

baths under the control of individual borough councils and was not promoted by London County Council except in a few swimming-baths attached to schools.

Institutes in London in 1960–1 were organized in such a way that classes for adolescents up to the age of twenty-one were generally separate from classes for adults. Table VII

TABLE VII

Physical Recreation Classes in London's Evening Institute

Selected activities showing numbers of classes for adults and adolescents.

ACTIVITY	NUMBER OF CLASSES	
	Adult	Adolescent (15–21)
Badminton	218	94
Table tennis	121	237
Football	114	227
Recreative gymnastics (men)	112	246
Recreative gymnastics and keep-fit (women)	192	37

shows how some of the activities made a different appeal to boys and girls and to men and women. Badminton was more popular among adults and football and table tennis more popular among adolescents. In the sphere of general physical training it appeared that men were less anxious to keep fit as they grew older but women were more anxious to do so. The subtle reasons for the differences shown in these figures would repay further investigations. Table VIII shows the change in demand and in provision of classes between 1950 and 1960.

One trend in modern sport which affects the young particularly but men and women of all ages to some extent is that of using sport for social contacts, especially contacts between the sexes. The trend is national rather than local. Many outdoor activities based on camps or youth hostels

enable men and women with a common sporting interest to
meet. There is also evidence that other sports fulfil the same
role. In the twenty-one years between 1935 and 1956 the
number of badminton clubs and the number of lawn tennis
clubs have both doubled. The fact that these games can be and

TABLE VIII

Physical Recreation Classes in London's Evening Institutes
The Changing Demand

Only those activities which, in 1960, commanded more than 100 classes
have been included.

ACTIVITY	NUMBER OF CLASSES	
	1950	1960
Dance of all kinds	1,134	661
Recreative gymnastics (men)	332	364
Recreative gymnastics and keep fit (women)	345	253
Table tennis	26	358
Football training	70	341
Badminton	6	312
Judo	50	228
Boxing	385	182
Weight-lifting	69	144
Fencing	86	103

often are played by men and women together accounts for
part of their increase in popularity.

Amid the complex pattern of sport in modern urban
and industrialized societies two features are discernible.
First is the radical, even revolutionary change of pattern that
has taken place since the end of World War II; its complexity
is now very much greater than before the war. The second is
the increase in the number of sports which are undertaken.
Hitherto the range of sports available to the mass of the
population has been extended without any of the older

established sports being squeezed out of existence. The expansion has been general but the future may well bring the contraction of some sports and perhaps their disappearance.

The present pattern of sport is difficult to delineate, but it is even more difficult to estimate whether the pattern satisfies the needs and aspirations of the people. Several reports of committees on youth and on sport in Britain have suggested that boys and girls between fifteen and eighteen, if they are not attending school or college, have inadequate opportunities for sport.[4, 5, 6] Since publication of the reports numerous regional surveys of facilities for sport and of the interests and desires of boys and girls when they leave school have been made.

The surveys have confirmed the inadequacy of some facilities for sport, especially indoor sport in Britain. They have also confirmed that the interests of boys and girls now range through the whole alphabet of sport from archery to wrestling, and are certainly not confined to games and sports which they have learnt at school. As they leave school they express their keenness to pursue judo, horse-riding, sailing, gliding, archery and many other sports which have not formed part of their formal education.

Disquieting facts which have been brought to light by several surveys are that very few boys and girls indeed make any plans or are helped to make any plans to pursue their favourite sport before they leave school, and that few adult organizations and clubs make serious attempts to lead young people into the adult world of sport. Football and swimming are notable exceptions to this general stricture. The governing bodies of these sports and many individual clubs have been assiduous in recruiting junior sections and junior teams. The women's hockey and netball associations have also made strenuous efforts to attract girls leaving school. Most of the girls themselves, however, appear to have interests in other sports and activities when they leave school and have not responded very readily to the encouragement of the associations. Ironically, the sports which they wish to pursue are not so well organized to receive them.

The problems of a changing pattern of sport are not confined to Britain. National Fitness Campaigns have been recently inaugurated in Canada, the United States and Australia. Massed movements in the communist countries and the coaching schemes and courses promoted in Africa and India suggest that all over the world sport is on the move. The movements whether spontaneous or artificially stimulated by political or commercial interests, have far-reaching implications. Some of the social and economic implications have already been sketched. The final chapter deals with some political ramifications of this growth.

BIBLIOGRAPHY

1. INTERNATIONAL UNION OF LOCAL AUTHORITIES, *The Concern of Local Authorities with Adult Education and Sport* (The Hague, 1960).
2. GALBRAITH, J. K., Chap. 24 *The Affluent Society* (Penguin Books, 1962).
3. FRAZER, IAN, reported in *The Guardian*, 24th July, 1962.
4. WOLFENDEN COMMITTEE, *Sport and the Community* (Central Council of Physical Recreation, London, 1960).
5. ALBERMARLE COMMITTEE, *The Youth Service in England and Wales* (Her Majesty's Stationery Office, London, 1960).
6. CROWTHER COMMITTEE, *15–18* (Her Majesty's Stationery Office, London, 1959).

See also

LONDON COUNTY COUNCIL, *London Development Plan–First Review* (1960).

MUMFORD, LEWIS, *The City in History* (London, 1961).
Contains a large and excellent bibliography of books and periodicals on urban life and urban planning in many different countries.

XIV

AMATEUR AND PROFESSIONAL

"I DON'T know what you mean by 'glory'," Alice said. Humpty Dumpty smiled contemptuously. "Of course you don't—till I tell you. I meant 'there's a nice knock down argument for you.'"

"But 'glory' doesn't mean 'a nice knock down argument,'" Alice objected.

"When I use a word," Humpty Dumpty said, in rather a scornful tone, "it means just what I choose it to mean— neither more nor less."

"The question is," said Alice, "whether you *can* make words mean so many different things."

"The question is," said Humpty Dumpty, "which is to be master—that's all."

For the amateur and the professional the world of sport is a looking-glass world. The masters are the governing bodies of sport in each country, the international federations, and above all, the International Olympic Committee. The words *amateur* and *professional* are used to mean just what each wants them to mean, and, as there is not one master but many, some curious anomalies have arisen.

Payment for coaching is permissible for amateurs in some sports but not in others, but the same person may want to coach or compete in more than one sport. A girl who accepts a fee for coaching hockey, however, is debarred from any swimming event held under the laws of the Amateur Swimming Association.

Another set of anomalies arises from the explicit statement

by some bodies that a professional in any sport is automatically a professional in the sports which they control, while other governing bodies are not worried by what a person does in any sport outside their jurisdiction. So it happens that a professional footballer may play tennis as an amateur but is debarred from all amateur competitions in swimming or athletics. Perhaps the most curious and least justifiable of all anomalies has been created by the Laws of the Rugby Football Union. The Union names seventeen possible acts of professionalism by individuals and sixteen acts of professionalism by club or other Rugby organizations. Among these acts is included "signing any form, whether amateur or professional, of the Northern Union or Rugby League ..." The Union makes no regulation about any other sport. A professional soccer player or a professional athletics coach therefore may play Rugby as an amateur, but an amateur Rugby League player is a professional in the eyes of the Rugby Union and strictly speaking is thereby a professional athlete, swimmer and boxer.

The looking-glass world of sport is not a happy one, nor an honest one. The Rt. Rev. C. M. Chavasse, until 1961 Bishop of Rochester, had in his youth played some games for a Rugby League Club. For the rest of his life he was debarred from helping any Rugby Union Club even in an administrative capacity and his offers of assistance were rejected. In Evening Institutes under Local Education Authorities classes in athletic training have to be called, and are called, recreative gymnastics so that the instructor may receive his fee without losing his amateur status as an athlete.

A semantic and historical examination of the terms amateur and professional may serve to explain the present situation and may suggest a way forward. The *Oxford English Dictionary* gives for *professional*, among other meanings, "that follows an occupation as his or her profession, life work or means of livelihood," as a "professional soldier, musician or lecturer"; "specially applied to one who follows by way of profession or business an occupation generally engaged in as a pastime," hence used in contrast with an *amateur*, as "professional cricketer." Disparagingly applied to one who makes a trade of anything that is properly pursued from higher motives, as a "professional politician." It is interesting to find sport and politics here in juxtaposition. Very few members of any community have been able to divorce their life's work from their means of livelihood, but those whose livelihood does not depend upon a particular trade or skill or profession are able to say that the occupations to which they do devote themselves are pursued from lofty motives. It is then an easy and almost inevitable step to say that those who make or supplement their livelihood from the same occupations pursue them from less lofty motives and have lost some of their integrity.

In the sixth century B. C. the free-born Greek who competed in the Olympic Games and other Panhellenic festivals spent several months in training and away from home. He was certainly supported by the community but not as an athlete. Athletics was one of several occupations to which he could devote himself. When Solon decreed early in the sixth century B. C. that any Athenian who gained a victory in the Olympic Games should receive 500 drachmae the professionalization of athletics had begun. It was not long before athletics became both a full-time occupation and a means of livelihood for some men. Then, indeed, they incurred the contempt of Aristotle, Aristophanes, Xenophon and Euripides. "Of all the countless evils throughout Hellas, none is worse than the race of athletes ... In youth they strut about in splendour, idols of the city, but when bitter old age comes they are cast aside like worn out cloaks" and again "Whoever helped his fatherland by winning a crown for wrestling or for speed of foot or hurling the discus or striking a good blow on the jaw . . . Crowns should be given to the good and the wise, to him who guides the city best, a temperate man and just, or who by his words drives away evil deeds putting away war and faction." In spite of the adulation of the athlete there was a social stigma upon the professional which derived from his falling away from the ideal of the ruling class rather than from his performing for profit. Professionalization was complete when the athlete was not only glad of the 500 drachmae and other rewards but could not live without them.

The dictionary meaning of the word *amateur* shows us the reverse side of the coin. Meaning literally *lover* the word was not in use much before the beginning of the nineteenth century. The *Oxford Dictionary* quotes this use of the word in 1803: "Amateur in the Arts is a foreign term introduced and now passing current amongst us to denote a person understanding and loving or practising the polite arts of painting, sculpture or architecture without any regard to pecuniary advantage." An implication of this statement is that some pursuits are "polite" and that others are "impolite." This distinction had recurred many times in sport long before the word amateur came to be used in the nineteenth century, but amateur gave a new form to an old concept. In the Renaissance the "courtier" had been the aristocratic ideal. In nineteenth-century England "gentleman" was the comparable idea. At first the word amateur was used to reinforce the word *gentleman*. "Gentleman amateur" had a social and class distinction like the term "gentleman commoner" which was used at Oxford and Cambridge colleges to distinguish certain undergraduates from other socially inferior students who were simply "commoners" or "scholars." In cricket the term "gentleman" was by itself sufficient to distinguish the upper class from the professionals or "players."

For an appreciable part of the nineteenth century gentleman

and amateur became convertible terms. A clear formation of this idea appeared in the rule laid down by the Henley Regatta Committee that no person should be considered an amateur oarsman who was or had been by trade or employment for wages a mechanic, artisan or labourer. In 1871 the committee declined to admit one of the local crews for the Wyfold Cup because they were not gentlemen amateurs by this definition.

For the first half of the century the question of pecuniary advantage from sport was not vital. In 1831 Oxford and Leander crews rowed at Henley for £200 a side and no-one thought that they thereby lost their status as gentlemen or as amateurs. Until 1861 the winner of the Wingfield Sculls took all the entrance fees of £5 an entry. Athletics meeting for gentlemen amateurs at Oxford featured wagers and money stakes. Eligibility to take part in these rowing and athletic events was determined by social status, and a tradesman or a labourer, despite the fact that he had never made—nor lost—a penny at sport, was still not accepted for amateur competitions.

The growth of sport during the nineteenth century extended far beyond the ranks of the gentlemen and as it did so the concepts of amateur and gentleman drifted apart. The Amateur Athletic Club in 1866 had adopted the Henley definition of an amateur but the Amateur Athletic Association in 1881 abandoned the clause which excluded mechanics, labourers and artisans. The Association, however, did rigidly legislate against pecuniary advantage. It was in the next year, 1882, that the Football Association passed Rule No. 16 forbidding payments to players other than expenses and "any wages actually lost." Other governing bodies of sport, many of which were founded about this time, thought it necessary to legislate about payments to players. Between 1870 and 1890 the amateur came to be defined no longer in terms of social status but in terms of rewards and payments. The professional, however, who in cricket and in other spheres of life had had a lowly social status, continued in that status and often had an added social stigma attached to his professionalism by the newly self-styled amateurs.

The various governing bodies of sport dealt with professional sport in different ways. For the Marylebone Cricket Club there was no serious problem. Professionals had long been employed by the Club and by county clubs. They had their contracts of service and the professional players were already firmly under the control of the M.C.C. Golf and horse-racing were in a similar position. The Football Association was at first, from 1863, concerned solely with the laws of the game, not with the status of players, but the popularity of the game, the gate money and the commercial promotions forced the Association to consider payment. It was decided to legalize and to control the professional game in 1885. The Rugby Union made exactly the opposite decision. The payment of players was forbidden even within the limits of loss of wages entailed by playing a particular game. Clubs which persisted in this practice were expelled and formed the nucleus of separate organizations, the Northern Union and later the Rugby League, which flourished in the north of England. The Amateur Athletic Association, the Amateur Swimming Association, the Amateur Boxing Association and other governing bodies which incorporated *Amateur* in their title rigidly excluded professionals from their activities and left them to legislate for themselves if they wished.

The nineteenth century legislators saw three dangers and had three corresponding fears. These fears were coloured by their social attitudes and prejudices but the dangers were not unreal. The first was that the payment of players would lead to some practices which were ethically questionable, such as poaching and touting, and to others which were certainly corrupt, such as the bribery of competitors and the arranging of results in advance. In the early years of the century important cricket matches had frequently suffered from the bribery of one or two outstanding players. Athletic meetings in midcentury, especially in the Midlands and the north, had become rife with bribery, the "arranging of races, impersonation of of athletes, and unpleasant disorder when the truth was uncovered." Many of the worst incidents were caused by the activities of professional gamblers rather than by professional competitors but it had often been difficult to distinguish the former from the latter.

The second danger was that performers who made sport their livelihood would so far outclass the amateurs that no competition between the two sets of performers would be possible. Some feared, too, that professionals would so dominate sport that amateurs would be discouraged and would drop out of these activities as they were thought to have done in the ancient world. The exclusion of amateurs from top-class competition, with one or two notable exceptions, came to pass in some sports. The early history of the F.A. Challenge Cup Competition provided a clear example. After 1882-3, eleven years from the start of the competition, no team of genuine amateurs reached the final.

The third danger was more subtle. Gentlemen amateurs had, for the most part, been educated in Public Schools and universities where conventions and etiquette on the playing fields were even more rigorously observed than the rules of the game. So, too, for that matter were the conventions about gambling and debts of honour. The Laws of Association Football still contain the phrase "ungentlemanly conduct," a phrase surviving from the nineteenth century which any players and officials of the day could interpret with a good measure of agreement. The gentlemanly spirit of the game was epitomized in a song "Forty Years On," written and composed for Harrow School in 1872. The boys sang the praises of "strife without anger and art without malice" on the football field. Amateur legislators felt keenly that working-class players could not maintain this spirit if they made a livelihood of sport. They felt, too, that in order to cherish this spirit they themselves must forego betting and competing for stakes in spite of the fact that these practices had not been found in the past to be incompatible with gentlemanly conduct.

Almost a century has now passed since the dangers of professionalism were faced by the legislative councils of sport. The record of corruption is remarkably meagre. Those cases which occasionally come before disciplinary committees or the courts of justice indicate the probity and honesty of most of the professional performers and paid officials. Professionalism may have many unsatisfactory aspects but corruption is not one of these. Indeed, there is some evidence and a great deal of suspicion that amateurs as active competitors, as officials and as committee members, have, in some sports, received payments and perquisites which are properly due to professionals. The charge of corruption might now be laid more justly at the door of the amateur than the professional. The danger needs facing afresh.

Unequal competition was seen as a real danger in 1880 but in the event its realization has not proved disastrous. In basket-ball the difference between the Harlem Globetrotters and a novice team on a baked mud court in Thailand or a youth centre in London is extreme. In spite of this massive inequality the world can boast between twelve and thirteen million basket-ball players and few people seem to have been discouraged by the supremacy of the professionals. The problem of unequal competition has been dealt with differently in different sports. In cricket the best gentlemen amateurs in the nineteenth century were able to spend as much time as they needed in order to bring their skill to a standard equal or superior to that of professionals. Neither W. G.

Grace nor Ranjitsinghi lacked time, energy or resources for this objective. After the 1914–18 war such opportunities were available to few amateur players and most of those who reached the top did so through the munificence of their nominal employers in granting the necessary time off. The next step was for county cricket clubs to find in their own service administrative employment for amateurs and the distinction between these and the professionals employed by the same club has become solely hierarchical. In November, 1962, the Advisory County Cricket Committee recommended that the distinction between amateur and professional should be abandoned and that thenceforward all who played the game should be known simply as cricketers.

The Football Association, finding that the cup competition was dominated by professionals, encouraged an amateur cup competition closed to professionals. Leagues and competitions all down the scale of ability also grew up. The Rugby Union resolution set itself against Rugby football becoming anything but a club game for part-timers. Broken-time payments and league and cup competitions were strictly forbidden. Those who wanted a different basis and perhaps a better standard of play in terms of sheer technical skill had to transfer their allegiance to the Rugby League and be outlawed by the Union. The Lawn Tennis Association allowed just the opposite to happen, so that the best amateurs received expenses which permitted them to become full-time rather than club players. Nowadays none but a full-timer, whether he be called amateur or professional, can win the bigger tournaments or gain international honours. Even in athletics and swimming the best performers are so dedicated that time and energy spent upon training is little less than would be expended by a professional. Many occupations cannot be reconciled with peak performance on the track. A Roger Bannister or a Gordon Pirie must subordinate his other pursuits to training in order to achieve success in international competitions. Bannister was not the first athlete to realize that being a medical student was compatible with modern training while being a qualified doctor was not.

In the communist countries all sportsmen are in theory part-timers even if for certain periods of training and competition their other occupation is abandoned. Yet even in planned societies this theory has been difficult to apply in practice. In November 1962 a *Pravda* investigation found sixteen professional footballers earning 200 roubles a month listed as farm workers and *Pravda* declared that there were "too many footballers who neither sow nor reap but are being kept at a cost of tens of thousands of roubles to the state."

In spite of careful and detailed legislation to cover professionalism, unequal competition has arrived in most sports but it is determined by expenditure of time not money. Inevitably, part-timers have found their own level and although this is some distance below the top, they have not been discouraged from competition.

What of the spirit of the game? Professionals have not noticeably shown themselves to be worse sportsmen than amateurs, nor have amateurs upheld the ideal of strife without anger or art without malice more assiduously than professionals, nor have part-time players behaved more like gentlemen than full-time players. There have been black sheep in every fold.

The International Olympic Committee faced the same fears and dangers in 1896 as did the governing bodies of sport but it did not have control over all sports all the time. On the contrary, it controlled between twelve and eighteen sports on a single occasion once every four years. The Committee depended upon those who governed and promoted different sports in different countries. In the early years of the Olympic movement the I.O.C. appeared to recognize its dependence and, having stated its ideal of amateurism, left to the governing bodies the task of ensuring the amateur status of the competitors. The Olympic Games in Berlin 1936 revealed to the I.O.C. that governments and other interested bodies could make the ideal and even the regulations a mockery. The I.O.C. later tried to be more amateur than the governing bodies. Rule No. 26 (1958) stated: "An amateur is one who participates and always has participated in sport solely for pleasure and for the physical and mental benefits he derives therefrom, and to whom participation in sport is nothing more than recreation without material gain of any kind, direct or indirect. *In addition*, he must comply with the rules of the International Federation concerned."

"In addition" was the key phrase for it implied that rules of International Federations did not conform to the I.O.C. rules on amateurism. Indeed, this was made plain in an amplification of Rule 26 given by the I.O.C.—

> Individuals subsidized by governments, educational institutions or business concerns because of their athletic ability are not amateurs. Business or individual concerns sometimes employ athletes or sponsor athletic teams for their advertising value. The athletes are given paid employment with little work to do and are free to practise and compete at all times. For national aggrandisement governments occasionally adopt the same methods and give athletes positions in the army or the police force or in a government office. They also operate training camps for extended periods. Some colleges and universities offer outstanding athletes scholarships and inducements of various kinds. Recipients of these special favours which are granted because of athletic ability are not amateurs.

The *I.O.C. Bulletin*, August, 1961, made the definition more concise and stated—

> An amateur is one who participates and always has participated in sport without material gain.

N

To qualify as an amateur it is necessary to comply with the following conditions—

(*a*) Have a normal occupation destined to insure his present and future livelihood.

(*b*) Never have received any payment for taking part in any sports competitions.

(*c*) Comply with the rules of the International Federation concerned.

(*d*) Comply with the official interpretation of this regulation

The official interpretation was given in September, 1962. It forbade ten different practices: money prizes, employment or promotion by reason of sporting performances rather than ability, employment as a cover for excessive training or competition, advertising, the intention to become a professional, payment for teaching or coaching, demanding money for a friend, excessive expenses and "the interruption of studies or employment for special training in a camp for more than three weeks." The memorandum giving this interpretation added: "So far as the Olympic Games are concerned these rules must be complied with even if they appear to conflict with the rules of any other body."

It is clear that the I.O.C. is now legislating not to ensure sportsmanship but to eliminate unequal competition. The I.O.C. desires the Olympic Games to be a festival of part-time performers, but it is difficult to see how this can be achieved unless the International Federations can define and enforce a "normal occupation" for all members and competitors. Hitherto they have not tried to do so and the Olympic Arena has been traversed by many athletes who have held "positions in the army" or have at least enjoyed a modicum of support from government, university or business concern during their training and competition.

What the future holds for the Olympic Games is a question for the next chapter: the conclusions of this one are that the

Olympic movement cannot be more amateur than the organizations which support it, and that the enforcement of part-time training and competition is likely to prove as difficult as the prevention of athletes receiving direct or indirect rewards for their prowess.

Beyond the Olympic corpus of sports, too, the amount of time spent by a performer on training and in competition is now seen to be more critical than the remuneration which he may receive. In Lawn Tennis the best amateur players of recent years have spent little less time in training and in competition than the recognized professional players. The amateur's expenses provide a means of livelihood year in and year out but by how much they exceed or fall short of the payments received by professionals is a matter for speculation. The time cannot now be long delayed when tournaments at Wimbledon, Forest Hills and elsewhere are thrown "open" to professionals. The logical development is for other governing bodies to recognize some "open" competitions, so that those who are good enough to compete with the best and who are willing to devote as much time and energy to training and competition as may be necessary to reach the summit may be paid from any reputable source during their competitive career without social stigma or disenfranchisement.

The present situation has been brought about very largely by the growth of international competition. International sport, therefore, will be discussed in the next chapter.

BIBLIOGRAPHY

For the rules governing amateur and professional status it is necessary to consult the handbooks of the International Federations or Governing Bodies of each and every sport. See also the bulletins of the International Olympic Committee especially for 1958 and August, 1961. For comment on the situation in the period 1950–60 see *Britain in the World of Sport* and *Sport and the Community* referred to in bibliographies to earlier chapters.

XV

SPORT, POLITICS AND
INTERNATIONALISM

In 1956 the armed conflicts in Hungary and Suez caused six nations to withdraw from the Olympic Games which were to be held in Melbourne, Australia. Mr. Avery Brundage, President of the International Olympic Committee commented: "By their decisions these countries show that they are unaware of one of our most important principles, namely that sport is completely free of politics." A superficial glance into the past is enough to show that very seldom has sport been free of politics. Certainly Baron de Coubertin did not see sport completely free of politics when he founded the modern Olympic Games. On the contrary, he hoped that sporting activities might improve the political relationships between nations. He addressed a circular to the governing bodies of sport in January, 1894, expressing the hope that every four years the athletic representatives of the world might be brought together and that the spirit of international unity might be advanced by the celebration of their chivalrous and peaceful contests. If sport was to influence politics it was hardly conceivable that the interaction should be in one direction only and that politics should have no bearing at all upon sport. The naïveté of Mr. Brundage's statement, however, must not be allowed to obscure the relationship between sport and politics which is felt to exist by many people besides the members of the I.O.C.

The relationship may turn bad in at least two ways, by too much interaction and by the debasement of either one of the two agents. The injection of too much sport into politics might reduce the most serious of human activities to puerilism, while the seriousness of politics, if carried into sport in too great measure, could destroy its playfulness and so change its very nature. Again, corruption in sport might lead to corrupt pressure being brought to bear upon local or national politicians which could harmfully affect the life of the community. The greater danger, however, is from corruption acting in the opposite direction. If the political life of a community is corrupt or is organized for unworthy or inhumane ends then it will hardly be possible for sport to remain unaffected; it will be harnessed, however loosely, to the same unworthy ends. The ideals of sportsmen may for a while pull the polity back or slow down its regress but observation of Germany in the 1930s and of South Africa in the decades since World War II suggests that sportsmen share the corrupt political and social ideas of their community in about the same measure as other citizens. Even if they do not share those ideals they tolerate them and their application to sport in order to be able to continue to play. There is at least one noble exception to this generalization which ought not to pass unnoticed. When in 1848, the German State of Baden attempted to implement a liberal constitution, Prussia and the other big states at once invaded Baden. The provisional government appealed for help to oppose the aggressors. The *Hanau Turnverein* sent three hundred armed gymnasts, who increased their number to six hundred *en route*. For a time they held out against the best-trained army in Europe. The end was inevitable. Some escaped to Switzerland. The rest were killed in action or shot as rebels after capture. The collapse of the political movement for a united, free and democratic Germany caused many gymnasts to flee across the Atlantic. In America they re-established their clubs. Their liberal ideals caused them to declare forcefully in favour of the abolition of slavery. They supported Abraham Lincoln politically and then enlisted in the armies of the North in considerable numbers.

Sport has certain characteristics which perhaps impel it more readily than other human activities towards an association with politics. Sport, especially competitive sport tends to identify the individual with some group and the individual welcomes this identity. Even the lone runner cannot escape his association with club or town, county or country. The member of a team inevitably sinks some of his individuality in the group. In the great age of sports development the extent to which the individual was submerged was an indication of merit in a game or sport. The young master in *Tom Brown's Schooldays* was made to say about cricket: "The discipline and reliance in one another which it teaches is so valuable, I think. It ought to be such an unselfish game. It merges the individual in the eleven; he doesn't play that he may win, but that his side may," to which Tom replies: "That's very true and that's why football and cricket, now one comes to think of it, are such much better games than fives or hare and hounds, or any others where the object is to come in first or to win for oneself and not that one's side may win."

The political significance of discipline, reliance on one another, and merging the individual in the group was not lost upon educators and statesmen in Victorian England. Furthermore, competitive sport fitted in well with the Victorian pattern of industrial and political rivalry. A belief in collisions, collisions of political parties, religious sects, industrial firms and teams of sportsmen was the light to illumine the broad road of social progress.

The merging of the individual in the group was not confined to the players themselves but to some extent was experienced by those who watched and those who shared a common club membership, a geographical location, or a racial affinity with the performers. In the later nineteenth century the growth of urban areas was so rapid and so amorphous as almost to smother the individual's sense of belonging to any group larger than the family, but on Saturday afternoons he could at least identify himself and his interest with those of eleven figures on the football field as he took his place on the terraces with thousands of others. Some transference of identity from local club to local government almost certainly helped the growth of civic sense and pride in cities such as Birmingham and Manchester. Local politicians who advocated measures to encourage or promote sport did so in the realization that they were helping the political development of their great towns.

In the United States the influence of sport on politics has been considerable. The line taken by German-American gymnasts has already been noted. In a broader sphere sport gave cohesion to a great variety of immigrants with different racial, religious and political backgrounds. It developed in America at about the same time as in Britain, in the latter part of the nineteenth century. Success quickly became an important matter of local prestige, and often the local representatives would be the high school or college; it thus united in rivalry different communities and townships. If the immigrants themselves retained some of their cultural isolation their sons found sport an easy avenue to the American way of life.

Success in sport was important to Americans and it is to their credit that in a community with a history of racial discrimination the racial complexion of the performer was not allowed to prevent his rise to the top in sport. He could represent his town, his state, his country if he were good enough. In boxing the negro Jack Johnson was heavyweight champion of the world from 1908 to 1915 at a time when the heroes of the American negro were almost all in sport because here could he meet and beat the white man on equal terms. Johnson himself in vaunting his superiority left a legacy of hatred. By 1937 the inarticulate and shy Joe Louis, the next negro heavyweight champion, was as beloved by white men as by negroes. In 1962 Floyd Patterson, the third of a great line, could write: "For myself I can truthfully say I feel no differently inside if I am fighting a white man or another negro." Later in that year he lost the world heavyweight title to the fourth negro to hold it, Liston.

In the Olympic Games many negroes have represented the United States with distinction. When in 1936 at the Olympic Games in Berlin Hitler refused to receive Jesse Owens because he was a negro after his great victories on the track, the action of the Führer was taken by Americans as an insult to them all.

North of the forty-ninth parallel the Canadians, with their federal constitution, provincial autonomy and large self-conscious minority population of French Canadians, have long experienced the lack of a sense of nationhood. In 1962 a government campaign for fitness and sport was launched by the Minister of National Health and Welfare who included this significant remark in his speech to Parliament: "Canadian participation in international competitive events is emerging as an important aspect of a growing spirit of nationhood."

Sport then has been found to be a cohesive agent and in countries where it is the policy of governments to keep a people divided as in South Africa or in Germany the community of interest in sport between different racial or political groups has been an embarrassment to the politicians.

In the planned societies of communist countries the interaction of sport and politics is deliberately carried a long way and the interaction is from politics to sport rather than in the opposite direction. At first, after the October revolution of 1917, the communist government in Russia took no official interest in sport. In 1925, however, sport was officially recognized and encouraged and in 1930-1 a number of tests in games and sports were instituted leading to the award of G.T.O. Badges ("Ready for Labour and Defence"). Sport was organized under an All Union Committee of Sport and

Physical Culture, a government organ responsible to the Council of Ministers of the U.S.S.R. From then onwards there was no suggestion in communist countries that sport was or ought to be "free of politics." On the contrary, sport and training for sport were used extensively for political education so that it became impossible to train as a coach without instruction in Marxism–Leninism and it was impossible to compete in a stadium great or small without being bombarded with the political slogans and ideas of the government of the day. Many sports meetings were organized by political organizations for political purposes.

In countries where sport is organized piecemeal by voluntary bodies and is, to all appearances, independent of political organization and indoctrination, it cannot be inferred that interaction between sport and politics does not take place. The difference is rather in the pattern of organization rather than in the presence of absence of interaction. The pattern of sport in Eastern and Western Germany exemplifies extremes of political organization.

All the German sports organizations were dissolved by order of the Control Commission after the war ended in 1945. In East Germany the government party then decreed that anyone who wished to take part in sport must do so as a member either of the new political youth organization (F.J.D.) or of the workers organization (F.D.G.B.). In 1948 the *Deutscher Sportausschuss* was set up with an avowed political aim. This was followed in 1952 by a State Committee for Sport and Physical Culture.

By contrast, in the Western Zone the *Deutscher Sportsbund* was set up in 1950 with the stated object of solving its problems without reference to party political, religious, racial or military considerations. The establishment of the *Sportsbund* was the result of efforts to find an organization which would enable sportsmen to govern themselves and pursue their interests without control or interference from the government.

Whatever may have been the differing patterns of organization of sport the interest of government organs in West Germany has been no less than in the East. In 1960 the German Olympic Association published a *Memorandum on the "Golden Plan" for Health, Sport and Recreation*. The Golden Plan was based on nation-wide surveys of sports facilities and asked for expenditure of £568,900,000 (6,315,000,000 D.M.) over fifteen years. The first four years were to be used in building up a combined federal and provincial government expenditure of £28,000,000 in direct grants to local communities. By 1961 grant aid from government sources already totalled £13,500,000 (150,000,000 D.M.) or forty-eight per cent of the target for 1964.[1]

To a greater or lesser degree the governments of all western European countries and many others besides now finance sport for their people, all but three of the European countries drawing the revenue to do so from football pools. In Great Britain annual direct aid to sport from the government in 1962 still amounted to no more than £670,000 and that sum was reached only after the Chancellor of the Exchequer had announced an increase of £200,000 on the original sum budgeted. The Wolfenden Committee Report, comparable in some ways to the German Golden Plan but much more modest, had asked for £10,000,000.

Undoubtedly the parsimonious treatment of sport by the British Government has been largely the result of firmly held beliefs that financial aid would involve government interference and that interaction between politics and sport must stop well short of this point. The same beliefs caused the Wolfenden Committee to reject vigorously the suggestion that there should be established a new Department of State called the Ministry of Sport. Yet the Ministry of Education is already, within limitations, a Ministry of Sport. It accepts or rejects all plans for new schools and colleges and so determines the facilities which are provided there for sport in school and out. It provides some of the money for their construction; it sets limits on expenditure on sport by local authorities, it makes a small grant, already mentioned, to voluntary organizations. It helps to finance the coaching schemes of governing bodies of sport and it helps to maintain three national recreation centres. Where sport is educational, and, broadly speaking, is being taught or learned rather than played for its own sake the Ministry of Education already exercises the functions of a Ministry of Sport by permitting, assisting, controlling, inspecting and, some would say, by interfering. When sport is educational it is considered worthy of political direction and some measure of control, but when sport becomes an end in itself it has so far ceased, in Britain, to be an activity which is appropriate for political support.

There have been three occasions when the political disinterestedness of the British Government has been breached. In 1927 the Air Ministry entered an official team for the Schneider Trophy Air Race. It did so again in 1929 and 1931. The race was at this time an international sporting contest, nothing more, and the intervention of the British Government in a sporting event preceded similar intervention by any other government of whatever political complexion. In 1954 the British Government once again broke its principle of non-participation in the world of sport. Roger Bannister had just become the first man to run the mile in less than four minutes. The Foreign Office sent him on a "good will" visit to the United States in order to improve Anglo-American relations.

In January, 1963, the British Prime Minister, having rejected the recommendation of the Wolfenden Committee for a Sports Development Council with funds to allocate, assigned to Lord Hailsham the task of co-ordinating the aid given to sport and recreation by different Government departments, such as the Ministries of Education, Health, and Housing and Local Government. It looked as if Lord Hailsham was to be in fact but not in name a Minister of Sport. At almost the same time there appeared on the horizon a cloud no bigger than a man's hand in the form of a small sum in the estimates of the Commonwealth Relations Office, a government Ministry, to meet a deficit which had been incurred by the British Empire and Commonwealth Games organization in participating in the Games in Western Australia in November, 1962. Whether this was a precedent of political significance was not clear at the time.

It is in the international sphere that the modern development of sport has most significant political implications, for it is here that the hazard to the true nature of sport is most acute and it is here that sport may make its most significant contribution to human welfare and sanity. The rise of international sport has been meteoric. The America's Cup race instituted in 1857 for friendly competition by yachts of different countries was probably the first modern international sporting contest of any consequence. Before the end of the century other international events had appeared, but at the first modern Olympic Games in 1896 there was only thirteen competing nations. In 1960 the number was eighty-four and it has been during the first sixty years of the twentieth century that international sport has come into real prominence.

One of the most considerable achievements has been the setting up of International Federations for the organization and control of individual sports. In sports where times and distances can be measured it soon became necessary to have a body to ratify records so that the claimant to a record could enjoy world-wide acceptance and recognition. In all competitive sports, however, as competitors from one country met those from other countries it became necessary to agree upon the rules and the eligibility of competitors to ensure even competition. The desire for this international competition at all levels of ability became so strong and so widespread that differences of language, of local practice, of social and educational background and of political outlook were not allowed to stand in the way of agreement on an essential basis for competition. Federations were set up for athletics, football, swimming, lawn tennis and many other sports. From the start the decisions of these bodies enjoyed a remarkable acceptance and obedience from constituent bodies all over the world. Whatever defects there may be in international sport there have at least been forms of democratic world government which have had tolerable success within their own limited jurisdictions. Since 1960 there has also been an International Council of Sport and Physical Education under the aegis of UNESCO which was already in 1962 beginning to bring together the international federations and organizations of teachers, coaches and leaders in a further limited world organization.

The desire for international competition is not confined to the richer and more highly developed countries but is shared by those countries which might be thought to be preoccupied with the basic needs for survival. A complete analysis of participants in the Olympic Games of 1952 was carried out in Helsinki and showed that one hundred and sixty competitors came from countries so poor that the annual *per capita* income was less than $100. Rich countries with a *per capita* income of more than $750 sent one hundred and ninety-four competitors.[2]

The best performers anywhere want to test their skill against the best from elsewhere, but because at international level the best performer merges some of his identity in the nation itself, whether he wants to do so or not, success in sport has political importance. This is true for the emergent nation as well as for the more highly developed countries. In February, 1959, the Indian Parliament debated a motion expressing concern at the deterioration of Indian sports, especially cricket. The motion was provoked by the previous failures of the Indian cricket team in the West Indies. One Member of Parliament suggested that no Indian team should be sent abroad for five years, to enable them to improve their standards. Canada, at the other end of the national income scale, launched a government campaign for fitness and amateur sport in 1962 in full recognition that "those who compete in the Olympic Games, the British Empire and Commonwealth Games, the Pan American Games and other international championship games are ambassadors of good will for Canada." The Prime Minister expressed the hope that the programme would add not only to the happiness and health of all people of Canada but to the international athletic prestige of Canada.

Direct intervention by a Head of State in sport because of its international and political significance took place in December, 1962. At that time in the United States disagreement between two rival governing bodies of sport, the Amateur Athletic Union and the National Collegiate Athletic Association, reached a climax. The Attorney-General failed to reconcile the two bodies. President Kennedy himself warned the American People in a Press conference on 12th December that the United States might not be represented at the next Olympic Games if the two factions refused arbitration. He said: "The governing bodies of these groups apparently put their own interests before the interests of our athletes, our traditions of sport and our country. The time has come for these groups to put the national interest first. Their continued bickering is grossly unfair. On behalf of the country and on behalf of sport I call on the organizations to submit their differences to an arbitration panel immediately."

These were strong words, but the political importance of the statement lay not so much in the words used as in the fact that directions were given by the President of the United States to voluntary sports organizations which realized less clearly than he did their own inescapable political responsibilities.

Communist countries have long openly regarded their sporting representatives as political emissaries who can do more than diplomats to recommend the communist philosophy and way of life to those who have not adopted it. East and west sportsmen, whether they like it or not, are "ambassadors of good will" and are under pressure to vindicate not merely their own prowess but the ideology of their country. There are few governments in the world which do not now accept the political importance of success in international sport.

The desire to win is sometimes so strong that sport cannot contain it; when this natural human desire is reinforced with political pressures it is small wonder that on occasion the structure of the sporting event bursts asunder. It was argued in an earlier chapter that play is an essential element in all sport if it is to retain its intrinsic value, and that play implies a defined area of unreality in which the rules of ordinary life are superseded for the time being. It is possible for very great tension to be built up in a game or contest without the illusion of unreality being shattered. Often, however, it is shattered in international sport. A game of ice hockey may develop into an unregulated fist fight as it did in the Winter Olympic Games at Squaw Valley in 1960. A game of water polo may turn into a bloodbath as it did in the Olympic Games in Melbourne in 1956. Cricket or football matches may be destroyed as sporting events by bottles thrown by spectators. On these occasions the illusion is shattered and the contest has all the aggression, humiliation and bitterness of real life.

On the other side of the balance sheet there are many

occasions when "strife without anger and art without malice" are maintained in the most intense competition. There have been numerous occasions at the Olympic Games when competitors from different ideologic blocks, even from countries in open hostility with each other have stood on the victor's rostrum, to receive their medals. Their nations' flags are flying, while the whole crowd stands to do honour to them. These moments and many honourable and friendly contests, unnoticed by the Press of the world, nevertheless enhance the dignity of man.

While competitors and spectators sometimes fail to sustain the unreality of sport, there are from time to time political forces which seek to destroy it. There is no reason in any sport why those who know and accept agreed rules and who have the necessary skill should not play together, yet in South Africa black and white races are not permitted to play together for fear of breaching the political doctrine of apartheid. In Europe, too, the political division of Berlin and the tension there in 1962 led to restrictions on movement between communist and non-communist countries which implied that no international sport would be possible between the two blocks.

In both these situations there was interaction from sport to politics as well as from politics to sport. The South African Olympic Committee was warned that it would be suspended by the International Olympic Committee if the South African government persisted with racial discrimination in sport. In the European situation the I.O.C. in March, 1962, stated that the Olympic Games would be held only in cities which would guarantee free access for all recognized teams. As no city in a country of the North Atlantic Treaty Organization would be permitted to admit East Germans, all these countries were debarred from holding the Olympic Games until they agreed to recognize the special and "unreal" nature of sport. The International Council for Sport and Physical Education urged UNESCO to try urgently to secure that the youth of the whole world and its officials might meet freely in sport. The Council cancelled its own general assembly which was to be held in Manila because the Government of the Philippines would not guarantee entry to delegates from communist countries.

The essential nature of sport is in danger internationally not only from restriction but also from domination by the two great power blocks, the U.S.A. and the U.S.S.R. It is inevitable in the present situation that they should be more than anxious for success and that this anxiety should be shared by their citizens and allies. In 1962 both global and local wars are likely to be suicidal ways of influencing people and winning support, and sport as a means of influence has assumed correspondingly greater political importance. The situation was analysed in essence by Arnold Toynbee in 1948. In *Civilization on Trial* he wrote: "Communism is a competitor [with the West] for the allegiance of that great majority of mankind that is neither communist nor capitalist, neither Russian nor Western but is living at present in an uneasy no man's land between the opposing citadels of two rival ideologies. Both nondescripts and Westerners are in danger of turning communist today, as they were of turning Turk four hundred years ago, and, though communists are in similar danger of turning capitalist—as sensational instances have shown—the fact that one's rival witch doctor is as much afraid of one's own medicine as one is afraid oneself, of his, does not do anything to relieve the tension of the situation.

"Yet the fact that our adversary threatens us by showing up our defects, rather than by forcibly suppressing our virtues, is proof that the challenge he presents to us comes ultimately not from him, but from ourselves."

It may be that sport will provide opportunities for all

O

people to meet this challenge but it may also happen that the Olympic Games and other top-level international competitions will change their character. There are indications that the U.S.S.R. will press for more and more sports to be included in the Olympic programme, for instance, parachuting, aerobatics and motor-racing, so that the Games become too vast for staging by any city other than one supported massively by a wealthy central government. The Russians may also press for the enlargement of the I.O.C. to such dimensions that it will be too unwieldy to exercise effective control and be a happy hunting ground for big powers. What could then happen is that the Olympic Games would be no more than a testing ground for two great political units. There would be no difficulty in training *élite* teams of participants whose efficiency and skill would be superb but who would cease to be sportsmen, just as the professional athletes of the Mediterranean arenas ceased to be sportsmen during the last five hundred years of the ancient Olympic Games. The competitions would be keenly contested but as predominantly political occasions they would cease to share with humbler events that playful unreality which is essential to sport. It remains to be seen whether the international bodies can so frame their regulations that a limit can be set to the political and financial exploitation of the best performers which will preserve their character as sportsmen. Most of these bodies have not so far shown signs of recognizing the problem and the International Olympic Committee, which has begun to see it, has not been markedly successful in finding a solution.

International sport is like an iceberg; a small part consisting of the Olympic Games and other world championships is seen, but most international contests go on unnoticed by Press or people. It is at this level that sport may have its greatest impact on world affairs. In his *Reith Lectures* in 1948

Bertrand Russell argued that the savage in each one of us must find some outlet not incompatible with civilized life and with the happiness of his equally savage neighbour. He suggested that sport might provide such outlets and that what was wrong with our civilization was that such forms of competition formed too small a part of the lives of ordinary men and women. Men must compete for superiority and it is best that they do so in contests which yield utterly useless results. This is not to say that the results do not matter. They matter supremely and if they do not they will not satisfy man or nation, but in sport victory is never for all time nor is defeat irreparable. The individual, the team, the nation, even the ideological block lives to fight another day.

The enormous growth of sport as a World-wide phenomenon may herald the birth of a new Olympic ideal and a new asceticism, an asceticism which looks to achievement and prowess in play as an end in itself. The final conclusion then is a paradox; sport, if it is pursued as an end in itself, may bring benefits to man which will elude his grasp if he treats it as little more than a clinical, a social or a political instrument to fashion those very benefits.

BIBLIOGRAPHY

1. MOLYNEUX, D. D., *Central Government Aid to Sport and Physical Recreation in Countries of Western Europe* (University of Birmingham, 1962).
2. JOKL, E. *et al.*, *Sports in the Cultural Pattern of the World* (Helsinki, 1956).

See also

COZENS, F. W. and STUMPF, F., *Sports in American Life* (Chicago, 1953).

INTERNATIONAL OLYMPIC COMMITTEE, *Bulletins*.

RUSSELL, BERTRAND, *Authority and the Individual* (London, 1949).

TOYNBEE, A., *Civilization on Trial* (London, 1948).

UNESCO, *The Place of Sport in Education* (Paris, 1956).

INDEX